Clinging to Hope

CHARLES R. SWINDOLL

CLINGING to HOPE

What Scripture Says about Weathering Times of Trouble, Chaos, and Calamity

TYNDALE
MOMENTUM®

A Tyndale nonfiction imprint

Visit Tyndale online at tyndale.com.

Visit Tyndale Momentum online at tyndalemomentum.com.

Tyndale, Tyndale's quill logo, *Tyndale Momentum*, and the Tyndale Momentum logo are registered trademarks of Tyndale House Ministries. Tyndale Momentum is a nonfiction imprint of Tyndale House Publishers, Carol Stream, Illinois.

Clinging to Hope: What Scripture Says about Weathering Times of Trouble, Chaos, and Calamity

Designed by Julie Chen

Published in association with Yates & Yates, LLP (yates2.com).

For information about special discounts for bulk purchases, please contact Tyndale House Publishers at csresponse@tyndale.com, or call 1-855-277-9400.

Library of Congress Cataloging-in-Publication Data

A catalog record for this book is available from the Library of Congress.

ISBN 978-1-4964-3538-5 (hc)
ISBN 978-1-4964-3539-2 (sc)

Printed in the United States of America

28 27 26 25 24 23 22
7   6   5   4   3   2

It is with much admiration and appreciation
that I dedicate this book to our two daughters:
Charissa Ann Gaither and Colleen Alissa Thompson.
Both of them have experienced numerous trials,
major disappointments, anguishing pain, and personal
heartaches. They have endured them all with great
grace and without losing their sense of humor.
Their mother and I love them deeply and
have a respect for them that knows no bounds.

Contents

Introduction

ONE THING I'VE NOTICED IN RECENT YEARS is that people have no margin. More and more, people from all walks of life seem to be living on the ragged edge of chaos.

- one financial crisis away from bankruptcy
- one blowup away from relational collapse
- one temptation away from moral failure
- one calamity away from emotional meltdown
- one illness away from physical breakdown
- one doubt away from apostasy

If chaos and calamity haven't found you yet, it's only a matter of time before they do. When—not if—that happens to you, where will you go for strength to endure—and for hope to carry on? None of us is exempt from the sudden trials and lingering tribulations of life. None of us.

Throughout 2020 and in the early months of 2021, it seemed everybody around me was dealing with their own calamities. They rolled in like a storm, stopped people in their tracks, and left their victims feeling helpless and even hopeless.

This reality hit hard while I was working on this very book. For about eight months, I lost sight in one eye. It was like a dust storm had blown in from the Texas Panhandle and obscured my vision. With one eye out of commission, the complications began to domino. My depth perception evaporated, and my night vision weakened. That made driving "exciting." Needless to say, my passengers suggested I give up driving for a while.

Others around me faced their own trials.

A very close friend of mine had to be rushed to the ER in an ambulance. It turned out he not only tested positive for COVID-19 but also had pneumonia, bronchitis, and strep! They got him to the hospital just in time, but that quartet of troubles could have easily done him in. I'm sure we could all close our eyes and picture people who didn't fare as well as my friend did.

Another friend of mine had his daily life come to a screeching halt during the infamous Texas "Icepocalypse" in February 2021. Historic below-freezing temperatures combined with lost power caused a pipe in his home to freeze and burst, flooding his downstairs. In the months it took to repair the damaged house and replace ruined property, everything in his life was put on hold. When something like that T-bones your life, you never really catch up, do you?

I know people who have spent their last cent of borrowed

optimism struggling against cancer. They suffered through aggressive chemotherapy, gathered prayer warriors around them who pleaded their case before God, and gripped hope with numb fingers while their suffering tried to rip that hope from them like a thief. Then they went in for a checkup and heard crushing news. Instead of the tumor shrinking, it metastasized. Perhaps you know all too well what that ride home was like or what dinner around the table felt like that evening. How easy to just give up on hope in days of deep disappointment and despair!

We're living in some tough days, friends. Sudden calamities hit us like nuclear meltdowns. The disaster itself is bad enough. But the aftermath and desolation can linger for years—even decades.

All of us are in desperate need of strength and hope. Life is difficult and demanding. It's often filled with pain, heartache, setbacks, and detours. Our disappointment in others saddens us. Scandals among those we respect shock us. Disputes in our families, churches, or workplaces demoralize us. When such troubles strike, they can be downright devastating.

But they don't have to be!

We can endure unexpected calamities. How? By taking our stand on the strong foundation of God's Word. When trials and tribulations rumble in like a fleet of bulldozers to demolish our lives, we can emerge from the rubble with a strong resolve to recover and rebuild. We don't have to settle for merely surviving; we can set our sights on thriving.

Our good, powerful, awesome God is inviting each of us to run to Him as our only strong tower, which can never teeter or topple.

In Him alone, we can find the strength and hope to endure.

CHAPTER I

WHEN TROUBLES COME AND STAY

Wisdom When You Face Long-Term Suffering

SOME TROUBLES COME AND GO—like occasional spring storms that keep you huddled at home for a day or so but eventually blow over. When the sun peeks through the clouds again, life goes on. No harm done.

Other times, though, troubles come and stay—like fierce hurricanes that not only ravage our lives but leave long-term wreckage in their wake. I know people in my home state of Texas who've suffered total loss from merciless Gulf Coast hurricanes, resulting in years of hardship and heartache from which they have never seemed to recover. We've all known days, weeks—even months or years—when our particular troubles refused to go away. Instead of waning with time, they intensified—or even multiplied!

Sometimes we feel like these immortal words of Shakespeare have been permanently inscribed on our lives: "a wretched soul, bruised with adversity."[1] Those "bruises" don't always show up on our skin. They may mar our relationships, crush our spirit, dim our hope, or drag us into the mire of emotional misery. Troubles that affect us this deeply don't just come and go. They get even more complicated.

The nineteenth-century Congregational preacher Joseph Parker used to tell young ministers that if they preached to suffering people, they would never lack for a congregation—because there's a broken heart in every crowd. This prevalence of sorrow didn't exist only in the Victorian era. It's commonplace in our own generation as well. Through decades of preaching, as I scanned row after row in my own congregations, I looked into smiling faces that masked deep sadness, unresolved conflict, or the latest crisis waiting to assail them again the instant they stepped out of the sanctuary.

The truth is, much of life is played in a minor key. And long refrains of prolonged troubles can feel like a two-year-old pounding on piano keys—no melody, no rhythm, no tempo. Just irritating, incessant noise.

Hurts and heartache, pain and disappointment, sickness and disability, criticism and failure can eclipse our happiness and cloud our hope for relief. It's hard enough to keep going when trials hit us from all sides—but when they come and refuse to go away, they can be devastating.

Entertainment may temporarily dull the edge of our suffering, but it offers no permanent answers. Travel may provide a nice break, but the nagging problems await us when the vacation is over. Busyness and distractions can push our troubles to the back of our minds, but when it's "quittin' time," they're ready to spring to the forefront again.

THE BIBLE'S REALISTIC PORTRAYAL

The Bible doesn't varnish over the rough realities of life with a thick coat of empty clichés. God's Word meets the truth of unbudging troubles head-on. I think of Job's description of life's hardships: "How frail is humanity! How short is life, how full of trouble! We blossom like a flower and then wither. Like a passing shadow, we quickly disappear" (Job 14:1-2). These aren't the words of some jaded cynic who just can't see the bright side of life. These words express the deep reality of suffering in a fallen world by a man who experienced more hardship and loss than you and I ever will.

Scripture speaks often of the bruises of adversity. In the Psalms, King David reminds all the faithful through the ages that "the afflictions of the righteous are many" (Psalm 34:19, NASB). In fact, if you browse just the Psalms, Proverbs, and Ecclesiastes, you'll notice a heavy emphasis on suffering, turmoil, trouble, and affliction.

In the New Testament, the apostle Paul, ever the realist, reminds us that "we are afflicted in every way" and "perplexed"—at a loss, confused (2 Corinthians 4:8, NASB). In the twisted maze of our prolonged troubles, we don't know which way to turn. How easy it is to feel lost!

As we're buffeted by tests and trials, the book of James offers help with profoundly realistic insight. When we open this letter, written to "Jewish believers scattered abroad" (James 1:1), most of us don't realize how deeply those first-century Jewish Christians were "bruised with adversity." Jews who had accepted Jesus as their long-awaited Messiah survived in a sort of no-man's-land. On the one hand, their own people wanted nothing to do with them because they appeared to have forsaken the law of Moses—*apostasy*!

On the other hand, the Gentiles despised them because they refused to sacrifice to the Gentile gods, observe their festivals, or worship at their temples—*blasphemy*! As a result, persecution broke out against those early Jewish Christians. Their businesses were boycotted. Their families were shunned. Their rights were revoked and their property confiscated. Not only were they deprived of their liberty and livelihoods, but many of them also lost their lives for choosing to follow Jesus.

James wrote his brief letter to these first-century wretched souls bruised by adversity, but his immortal words continue to speak to all of us who are bruised by various troubles that come and stay. Offering encouragement and comfort, James answers four questions about troubles, which are as relevant today as they were in the first century:

- First, who will face troubles?
- Second, what is the purpose of troubles?
- Third, how do we handle troubles?
- Fourth, when we've handled troubles correctly, what then?

WHO WILL FACE TROUBLES?

As James begins his discussion of troubles, notice his word choice: "*when* troubles . . . come your way" (James 1:2, emphasis added). His use of "when" here tells us *troubles are inevitable* for all of us. James doesn't say "*if* troubles come" or "when troubles come to somebody else" or "in the unlikely event that a trouble or two crosses your path."

It's when, not if.

James has both feet in reality, and he wants his brothers and sisters in Christ, including you and me, to know that troubles are inescapable.

Because of our human nature, though, we don't want to believe it. Whole heresies have been founded on the falsehood that troubles are only for weak or disobedient Christians, people who don't have enough faith to thwart suffering, sickness, trials, and troubles. Then, when those inevitable troubles do come (and they always do), guess whose fault it is? Yours, they say, because you didn't have enough faith. Or you had too much sin in your life. Or you failed to confess your troubles away with a powerful "word of faith."

Thankfully, most of us haven't been hoodwinked into that name-it/claim-it, health-and-wealth heresy. But a common characteristic among believers is the desire to find a more pleasant detour around trials or even to run away from them. We may seek to fill our lives with enough busyness to muffle the noise. Or we may try to drink or smoke difficulties away or turn to pills or other man-made means of numbing the pain.

But we can't get away from troubles.

We may not have the same struggles as someone else, but we will have struggles of some sort. That's why James says, "Dear brothers and sisters, when troubles *of any kind* come your way" (emphasis added). The word translated "of any kind" is the Greek term *poikilos*. It means "diverse, variegated, many-colored." The NASB translates the term as "various."

The word *poikilos* always makes me think of polka dots, and that's a good illustration of what troubles are like. Troubles come in all sizes and colors. Some are irksome and irritating, others deep and dangerous. Some come and go without warning, like pestering flies; others burrow deep into our lives, like invasive parasites. Some mar our bodies with pain and paralysis; others weigh on our minds, causing relentless anxiety.

Odds are, you don't have to think long to come up with a list of troubles. You may have experienced anything from car trouble or broken bones to job loss or financial difficulties, from rebellious children or marriage failure to chronic illness or betrayed trust. And the feelings that accompany these troubles—feelings of rejection, insecurity, guilt, shame, depression, worry, rage, and envy—can cast long, lingering shadows over our lives. Regardless of the severity or duration of our troubles, we will all experience them.

WHAT IS THE PURPOSE OF TROUBLES?

When the inevitable troubles of various kinds come, remember the second truth about them—*they have a purpose*. We're not just tossed into the crowd and left to fend for ourselves as God runs the world from a distance. The various troubles that occur are all part of His plan. When we accept this, we can view them as opportunities for growth.

Notice what James says: "When troubles of any kind come your way, consider it an opportunity for great joy" (1:2). A trial is a faith test that exercises your endurance, not to break you but to strengthen you (see verse 3). So James says to let that endurance grow (verse 4). Don't look for an escape hatch. Instead, lean into God's plan and learn from the trial. Let it water your roots so you can grow deeper in your relationship with Him.

As I've looked back over the decades of my life, I've learned the value of yesterday's pain. Our trials are where the most important lessons are learned. Sometimes we learn from our own failures or through difficult situations we ourselves have caused. Often we grow from falling prey to others' poor choices or circumstances beyond our control. When we value the lessons learned through our trials, they will help us to become mature. They all have a purpose. They are all part of our loving heavenly Father's plan to conform us to the image of His Son.

Recognizing that troubles have a purpose is much better than always asking, "Why did this happen? Why me? Why now?" Instead, we can ask much more fruitful questions: "What can I learn from this about God's grace? About the love of His Son? About the comfort of the Holy Spirit? What important truth is God teaching me at this point in my journey?"

When we shift our focus from "why" to "what," we can begin to face the inevitable troubles of life as opportunities for growth and great joy.

HOW DO WE HANDLE TROUBLES?

The third question about troubles flows from James's answer to the first two. We can't avoid the various troubles in life, but we can accept that God has purposed them for our good. We're to view them as opportunities for rejoicing in the work He's doing in our lives—challenging us so He can change us.

All that's true, but how do we endure the process of trial and change? How do we keep from being overwhelmed and swept away by troubles? How do we keep the trials designed for our good from crushing us? When we look more closely at James's words, we see four important terms woven into the fabric of this tough passage: *consider*, *know*, *ask*, and *endure*. These words will help us answer the question of how to handle troubles.

Consider

In the original Greek text, verse 2 begins not with "troubles" and not even with "brothers and sisters." It begins, literally, "all joy *consider*." In Bible times, Greek word order didn't matter as much as in modern English, so writers often moved certain terms or phrases to the beginning of a sentence for emphasis. So, circle the word *consider* in your Bible. Underline it. Highlight it. That's James's emphasis: "Consider it an opportunity for great joy."

The term *joy* doesn't refer to laugh-out-loud hilarity. That would clearly not be an appropriate response to trials and calamities. *Joy* refers to a deep-seated, positive spirit, a calm, conscious resolve of hope in the midst of circumstances that would normally push people toward despair. This can come only when you *consider* that God has a reason for allowing these troubles in your life.

Note that *consider* in James 1:2 is a command. It's not something that comes naturally. You have to consciously choose to do it. And it doesn't come easily. It takes an act of the will.

Don't just acknowledge the truth about God's purpose in our trials; ponder it. Don't just nod your head in agreement; lean into it with your whole heart. Remind yourself, "There's a reason for this difficulty. Through this, I'll get to know God better. I'll get to know myself better. Maybe I won't know exactly how God is working things out for my good and His glory, but I'm going to regard it as true." Then remind yourself again. Consider.

Know

Next, James says, "For you *know* that when your faith is tested . . ." (1:3, emphasis added). What do you know? You know that this lingering trouble is deepening your faith, increasing your endurance, enhancing your character, sharpening your discernment, and building your maturity (see verse 4). When you know this, you're better able to consider your difficulties with a positive spirit.

But let's be honest. We always want the fruits, but we seldom want the fertilizer. We want to reap the wares, but we don't want to pluck the weeds. We want a bountiful harvest of spiritual growth, but we don't love the toil of tilling the rock-hard soil. This is why James wants us to keep at the forefront of our minds the outcome of this trouble. It's a testing ground for our faith.

This reminds me of the words of twentieth-century British journalist, soldier, and spy Malcolm Muggeridge. In the middle of his life, he converted from agnosticism to Christianity. Reflecting on a long life of hardship, heartache, and pain, he wrote:

> Contrary to what might be expected, I look back on experiences that at the time seemed especially desolating and painful with particular satisfaction. Indeed, I can say with complete truthfulness that everything I have learned in my seventy-five years in this world, everything that has truly enhanced and enlightened my existence, has been through

affliction and not through happiness. If it ever were to be possible to eliminate affliction from our earthly existence by means of some drug or other medical mumbo jumbo . . . the result would not be to make life delectable, but to make it too banal and trivial to be endurable.[2]

It is in our trials that we reap the greatest spiritual harvest. Knowing this truth will help us to endure the challenges we face.

Ask

The third word: *ask*. James continues by saying, "If you need wisdom, *ask* our generous God" (1:5, emphasis added). This verse isn't starting a new topic. James is still talking about how we can handle the various inevitable troubles we experience. In order to consider the truth about God's purposes in our trials and to know with confident hope that these trials are happening for our good, we need wisdom from above.

You may have noticed that worldly wisdom will tell you that it's all your fault. Or that it's somebody else's fault. Or that God is out to get you. Maybe you've even heard the world say that He doesn't care about you—or worse, that He doesn't even exist!

But divine wisdom helps us see through those smoke screens. We need His wisdom to see the truth. We're not born with that kind of insight. We don't inherit it. We can't take a course in it at school, in college, or even at seminary.

True wisdom comes from the mind of God, through a relationship with His Son—who is wisdom incarnate—by the power of the Spirit of wisdom and truth. And our triune God is not a stingy guide rationing out wisdom one precious drop at a time. He wants to lavish it upon us at those times we need it most.

All we have to do is ask.

I would define the wisdom of James 1:5 as "looking at life from God's point of view." Not the point of view of the evening news. Not the twisted perspective of your Facebook or Twitter feeds. Not the noisy outrage of the public square or political boxing ring. And certainly not the popular opinions of the latest Hollywood darlings.

We find true wisdom in God, who "will not rebuke you for asking" (James 1:5). Instead, He gives His insight to those who ask with unwavering faith (verses 6-8). He opens our eyes to the wisdom of His inspired Word, impressed upon our hearts and minds by His Holy Spirit.

When troubles come and stay, we need to drop to our knees and ask God for the wisdom to handle them. We can pray something like this: "Lord, I'm in a mess, part of which I caused and part of which I didn't. It has brought loss, heartache, feelings of failure, and disappointment to me and to others. I need You to help me see through Your eyes what I can't see through my own. Help me, Lord, to grow through this experience, to look at these troubles from Your perspective. By Your grace, let me ponder it rightly and gain a proper understanding of it. I desperately need Your wisdom, because I don't have it in myself."

When you ask for wisdom with an honest and sincere heart, you can trust God to answer.

Endure

James uses one more word to help us rise above our troubles: *endure*. The Greek noun *hypomonē*, or "endurance," appears twice in the passage: "You know that when your faith is tested, your endurance has a chance to grow. So let it grow, for when your endurance is fully developed, you will be perfect and complete, needing nothing" (James 1:3-4).

The term comes from two Greek words, *hypo*, meaning "under," and *menō*, meaning "to abide" or "to remain." It implies persevering under extreme difficulty, as a mule or donkey laden with a heavy burden holds up under the weight. We're called to "remain under" the burden of our trials for as long as God has us on that leg of the journey.

But don't fret! God doesn't toss a ton of trouble on us, coax us with a prod, and shove us on our way through life. He provides all the strength we need for the trek. Just as God is the source of wisdom to understand hardships (James 1:5), He's also the source of our strength to endure them (see Romans 15:5). In Colossians 1:11, Paul petitions God on behalf of his readers, "We also pray that you will be strengthened with all his glorious power so you will have all the endurance and patience you need."

We're not on our own. We endure because He gives us grace to endure.

Consider . . . Know . . . Ask . . . Endure

These four words have the power to change everything.

We *consider* that God has a purpose in our troubles.
We *know* He's cultivating character and motivating maturity.
We *ask* for wisdom to see beneath the surface of the trials.
We *endure* through the strength that comes from Him.

Rather than grousing and complaining about our troubles and making other people miserable in our pursuit of pity, we persevere because we find contentment in the fact that a good Father is at work. He's on our side. And when we endure those trials that come and stay, we learn significant lessons we could never have learned any other way.

Pulitzer Prize–winning columnist Charles Krauthammer's last book, released after his death in 2018, is titled *The Point of It All.* While he was attending Harvard Medical School, a diving accident left him paralyzed from the neck down. Despite the challenges of his condition, Krauthammer finished his degree in psychiatry and lived a long, fruitful life of public service—as a psychiatrist, speech writer, journalist, author, and nightly news commentator. He was also a husband and father.

At the end of the book, his son, Daniel, wrote a touching eulogy—lessons learned from his father that illustrate the truth of James well: "Don't be defined by what life throws at you and you cannot control. Accept the hand you are dealt with grace, and then go on to play that hand as joyously and industriously and vigorously as you can."[3]

That's how we handle troubles.

WHEN WE'VE HANDLED TROUBLES CORRECTLY

James 1:12 offers two specific promises for those who have handled troubles as they should—one for now, the other for when we stand before our Lord to receive our eternal rewards.

First, right *now*, "God blesses those who patiently endure testing and temptation." There's our word again—endure. Not only does God grant us the strength to endure, but He also rewards us for that endurance. What grace! Today, right now, we can be blessed with a sense of inner peace even in the midst of troubles that don't seem to quit. When hardships multiply, grace abounds. When our attempts to fix our problems fail, grace keeps us standing. When we handle trials God's way rather than through our own efforts, we receive a sense of contentment, satisfaction, patience, and even deep joy. We realize God is nurturing our character with the long view in mind.

Then, *afterward*, we "will receive the crown of life that God has promised to those who love him" (James 1:12). What a promise! James calls us to lift our eyes from our present troubles and to look beyond the horizon, beyond the return of Christ, when we will stand before our Lord and Savior—not to receive condemnation and castigation, but commendation and compensation. As the Scripture affirms, "We must all appear before the judgment seat of Christ, so that each one may receive compensation for his deeds done through the body, in accordance with what he has done" (2 Corinthians 5:10, NASB).

Of course, "there is no condemnation for those who belong to Christ Jesus" (Romans 8:1). Yet, the work we perform for Christ in this earthly life does determine the rewards we receive when we stand before Him. Elsewhere Paul notes that our contributions to building up the body of Christ will be tested, like the quality of earthly building materials are tested by a fire: "The fire will show if a person's work has any value. If the work survives, that builder will receive a reward. But if the work is burned up, the builder will suffer great loss," though "the builder will be saved" (1 Corinthians 3:13-15).

Scripture uses the image of *crowns* to describe the future rewards of commendation for those who have labored for Christ. It mentions five specifically:

- A crown that will last forever (1 Corinthians 9:25, NIV)
- The crown of exultation (1 Thessalonians 2:19, NASB)
- The crown of righteousness (2 Timothy 4:8)
- The crown of life (James 1:12)
- The crown of glory (1 Peter 5:4)

Together these paint a powerful picture of a magnificent eternal destiny—physical tokens of those longed-for words, "Well done, my good and faithful servant" (Matthew 25:21). Handling troubles correctly is so significant that James mentions a specific crown of reward for it.

What a great word of hope for us all! If we learn to handle life's trials correctly, we'll experience God's blessings now—and receive God's rewards in eternity.

BEYOND THE BRUISES

We began by talking about "wretched soul[s], bruised with adversity"—a Shakespearean phrase apt for all of us at some point in our rough-and-tumble journey through life. I'd like to revisit that description in light of everything we've seen in James's honest and encouraging look at the various troubles we'll encounter.

If we embrace James's insightful principles regarding trials, if we ask God for wisdom to think about them properly, and if we rely on His power to endure them, we can go from wretched souls bruised by adversity to wise souls matured through adversity. By God's grace, I've experienced this kind of transformation in my own life. It's what I would hope for you, as well.

God knows your circumstances right now. He knows the various troubles you're experiencing—those that come and go and those that come and stay. In fact, when God the Son walked this earth, He endured the same kinds of trials, temptations, and sufferings we endure. Because God calls us His children (see John 1:12; Romans 8:14), I can assure you that He will faithfully lead you by the hand through your darkest valley (see Psalm 23:4).

James 1:12 promises a "crown of life" to "those who love him." You know what else God promises to those who love Him? Romans 8:28 says, "We know that God causes everything to work together for the good of those who love God and are called according to his purpose for them."

Let me urge you, on the basis of God's Word, to trust that He is working in your troubles for your good. Let the lingering trial run its course. Seek His mind as you ask for the wisdom only He can give. Know that He is at work to bring you a depth of character you would otherwise miss.

CHAPTER 2

WHEN SUFFERING LEAVES ITS MARK

Wisdom When You Don't Find Healing

IN FEBRUARY 1974, my wife, Cynthia, and I were returning on a flight from Dallas to our home in Southern California. We had spent almost a week in Texas celebrating the fiftieth anniversary of Dallas Theological Seminary. Several other ministers and Christian workers who had participated in the event were on the same plane, a 747 jumbo jet. Our coach section was half empty, so some of us were making a little noise with laughter and lighthearted conversation.

After a while, we noticed a family in our section sitting in almost morbid silence. When we walked over to meet them, we learned their tragic story. The father of the family had been diagnosed with stage IV cancer. He was on that flight, lying down in the rear section of the plane, too weak to sit up on his own.

His wife told us the story of how they had ended up on that plane to Los Angeles. When the doctors told them nothing more could be done, they hung their hopes on a desperate act of faith. They had seen a so-called "faith healer" on TV and had withdrawn the entire contents of their bank account to exchange for an anointing with "healing oil" and a "prayer of faith" for a miraculous healing. They were on their way to meet with her now.

After telling their story, the wife asked us, "What do you all believe about faith healing?"

My colleagues suddenly became unusually quiet. For some reason they looked at me as if I were the appointed spokesperson for the group.

So, with as much sensitivity and compassion as I could muster, I told her that I certainly believe God can and does heal people naturally and supernaturally. I believe the Lord our God is a miracle-working God. Nothing is impossible for Him. But I don't see biblical justification for so-called divine healers or faith healers. Her shoulders slumped. Tears filled her eyes. I knew this wasn't what she wanted to hear.

In the short time we had on that plane, I was able to explain just a little of what the Bible teaches about healing. I prayed with her and even gave her my name and home phone number. I asked her to call me if her husband was miraculously healed as a result of bringing him to this TV healer. She assured me that she would call me immediately with the good news.

I never heard from her or her family again.

A COMMON SOURCE OF QUESTIONS

Over the years, I've often thought of my conversation with the woman on that flight from Dallas to Los Angeles—and of the thousands of people like her. They put all their hopes and dreams—and sometimes large sums of money—into an act of desperate faith to receive a miraculous healing.

As a pastor, I have ministered to some of those who have been burned by charlatans claiming God promised something He never did. Sometimes these disillusioned people are angry at themselves for being taken in by the false promises. Sometimes they're angry at the counterfeit faith healers. And sometimes they're angry at God because their loved one wasn't healed. Most remain confused. Where do we turn in God's Word to counter the misplaced confidence in so-called faith healers without losing confidence in the real promises of a good, all-powerful, loving God?

When suffering makes its mark, several vital questions become paramount in people's lives. Especially if that suffering comes from ongoing, anguishing pain, debilitating injuries, or a terminal disease. Does God heal people today? If so, does He do it through people with a supernatural gift of healing—divine healers or faith healers? Should everyone believe God for healing? What about the use of medicine or "natural" treatments?

These are all important questions, but perhaps the biggest question is why? Why does God allow suffering to remain and leave its mark on our lives? We will set this question aside for a moment to first consider what God's Word teaches about divine healing.

FIVE FOUNDATIONAL FACTS ABOUT HEALING

Our views on divine healing must rest on solid biblical theology. Not on personal opinions and testimonies. Not on popular preachers' sensational claims. Not on feelings. We must rest our faith and hope on Scripture. So, let me lay out five foundational facts drawn from God's Word. Picture them as five pillars driven deep into the soft ground of our unreliable opinions, emotions, and experiences. They will provide you with a solid foundation for building a trustworthy theology of suffering.

There Are Two Categories of Sin

The first foundational fact is that there are two categories of sin—*original sin* and *personal sins*. Original sin refers to the condition in which we were all conceived. Our parents were sinners, their parents were sinners, and their parents' parents were sinners—all the way back to Adam and Eve. Every human who ever lived—except Jesus—inherited this sin nature from our original human ancestors, Adam and Eve. As a result of their disobedience in the Garden of Eden, they fell from their innocent, unblemished condition to a condition of mortality, spiritual death, and condemnation. Every person descended from them (including you and me) is wrapped up in that same condition. The result is summed up by Paul in Romans 3:9-10: "All people, whether Jews or Gentiles, are under the power of sin. As the Scriptures say, 'No one is righteous—not even one.'"

The second category is personal sins. These are individual acts of wrong we all commit because of our sin nature. Think of it this way: because of original sin (the root), we commit personal sins (the fruit). Romans 3:12-16 describes some of these fruits: "'No one does good, not a single one.' 'Their talk is foul, like the stench from an open grave. Their tongues are filled with lies.' . . . 'Their mouths are full of cursing and bitterness.' 'They rush to commit murder. Destruction and misery always follow them.'" In fact, "everyone has sinned; we all fall short of God's glorious standard" (3:23).

This distinction between original sin and personal sins takes us to Psalm 51, a psalm of repentance David wrote after his adulterous affair with Bathsheba. In verse 1, David cries out to God for mercy: "Because of your great compassion, blot out the stain of my sins." That's a reference to David's personal sins—his illicit relationship with Bathsheba; the plot to have her husband, Uriah, killed on the battlefield and the resulting hypocrisy and lies; not to mention the heart-level sins of pride, discontent, and lust that fueled his actions. For all these, David asks the Lord's forgiveness. Yet David also goes to the root of the problem—his original sin. In verse 5, he says, "For I was born a sinner—yes, from the moment my mother conceived me."

We commit personal sins because we have a nature that is addicted to sinfulness. This won't change until after this mortal life, when we have a new nature that comes with a glorious, resurrected body (see 2 Corinthians 5:1). But as long as we're on this earth, breathing earthly air, we carry within us this fallen nature as a result of original sin. So, we classify sin in two ways: original sin and personal sins. We need to have these two categories of sin in mind before we broach the subject of sickness and healing.

Original Sin Introduced Sickness and Death

The second foundational fact relates specifically to original sin and its effects. Not only did the sin of Adam and Eve result in all humanity's having a sin nature, it also introduced suffering, sickness, and death to the world. If Adam and Eve had never disobeyed God by eating from the tree of the knowledge of good and evil (see Genesis 2:16-17; 3:6), none of these effects of sin would have entered God's good creation—or your life and mine. But upon eating the fruit, they immediately died spiritually and began the long, agonizing process of dying physically. Romans 5:12 says, "When Adam sinned, sin entered the world. Adam's sin brought death, so death spread to everyone, for everyone sinned."

Not only that, but creation itself feels the distressing blows of sin and death. Later in the book of Romans Paul writes, "All creation was subjected to God's curse. But with eager hope, the creation looks forward to the day when it will join God's children in glorious freedom from death and decay. For we know that all creation has been groaning as in the pains of childbirth right up to the present time" (8:20-22). Note what Paul says: the "curse" that entered the very fabric of creation involves "death and decay."

Sometimes Personal Sin and Sickness Are Related

The third foundational fact is that sometimes there is a direct relationship between my personal sin and my sickness. Though everything I said about suffering and sickness as a general result of the Fall and original sin is true, sometimes a person becomes sick as a result of sin in their lives. Several examples in Scripture bear this out. In Psalm 32, David writes, "When I refused to confess my sin, my body wasted away, and I groaned all day long" (verse 3). Look at those words carefully. David's acts of sinfulness caused his body to suffer. Perhaps you have felt the emotional turmoil that such guilt can cause. It twists our insides, churns our stomachs, keeps us up at night, stresses us out. Those natural effects of unconfessed sin can do a number on us physically. David calls this emotional and physical suffering God's "hand of discipline" (verse 4)—a direct relationship between personal sins and sickness.

Similarly, consider David's honest words in Psalm 38:

O Lord, don't rebuke me in your anger
    or discipline me in your rage!
Your arrows have struck deep,
    and your blows are crushing me.
Because of your anger, my whole body is sick;
    my health is broken because of my sins.
My guilt overwhelms me—
    it is a burden too heavy to bear.
My wounds fester and stink
    because of my foolish sins.
I am bent over and racked with pain.
    All day long I walk around filled with grief.
A raging fever burns within me,
    and my health is broken.
I am exhausted and completely crushed.
    My groans come from an anguished heart.

PSALM 38:1-8

To prevent us from thinking this kind of divine discipline was only an Old Testament phenomenon, look at Paul's words in 1 Corinthians 11:29-30 regarding unworthy participation in the Lord's Supper: "If you eat the bread or drink the cup without honoring the body of Christ, you are eating and drinking God's judgment upon yourself. That is why many of you are weak and sick and some have even died." God's judgment in that matter resulted in sickness and even death.

In each of these situations, sickness came as a result of personal sins. In each case the sinner was aware of the sin, because their deep guilt ate away at them. Or, in the case of the New Testament example, they willingly and knowingly engaged in serious sins against their fellow brothers and sisters in the church and against God Himself. These examples show that on occasion, personal sin and sickness are related.

Sometimes Sin and Sickness Are Not Related

We now have three hard teachings in place. We understand that there are two types of sin, that original sin brought sickness and death into the world, and that our personal sins and sickness are sometimes related. We're ready for the fourth foundational fact: sometimes our personal sins and our suffering and sickness have no relationship to each other. Just by living in this world marred by decay, subject to suffering, and cursed with death, we're bound to experience those harsh realities. Even if we never commit heinous sins deserving of capital punishment, we will experience death. Even if we eat healthy foods and exercise regularly, we'll suffer from sickness, accidents, and injuries. Not because we've personally done something to attract God's ire, but because we live in a world contaminated by sin and death.

For a biblical example of this, turn to John 9—the story of a man born blind. Jesus' disciples ask Him a question that has nagged humanity for millennia: Why? Look closely at their question: "Why was this man born blind? Was it because of his own sins or his parents' sins?" (verse 2). The disciples' narrow theology assumes the blind man's condition must have come upon him either (a) as a result of the man's personal sins, or (b) as a punishment for his parents' sins. Those young disciples had been trained in their synagogue schools with the "you-get-what-you-deserve" theology of the Pharisees.

Look how Jesus answers: "It was not because of his sins or his parents' sins. . . . This happened so the power of God could be seen in him" (verse 3). In other words, to the disciples' question, Jesus responds with "None of the above." Sometimes, sin and sickness aren't related.

The disciples' this-or-that options shouldn't surprise us. People are often so caught up in the disability, injury, or illness and so concerned about the question Why? that they forget that God always has a bigger purpose beyond the suffering. In this case, the man born blind would become a living testimony to the power of God.

If we want to trace the relationship between sin and sickness further, we can look at Exodus 4:11. When Moses complains to God about his own disability in speaking—perhaps due to a speech impediment—God responds, "Who makes a person's mouth? Who decides whether people speak or do not speak, hear or do not hear, see or do not see? Is it not I, the LORD?" Clearly, God's sovereignty extends even over our disabilities.

I know this can be a delicate subject, wrought with all kinds of controversy. People take it personally. You yourself may know somebody suffering from a disability through no fault of their own. Perhaps you have trouble seeing how God could use that to His glory and their good.

Unless God Himself reveals His purpose—and He rarely does

so—we need to trust Him when we face sickness or disability. Trust His goodness. Trust His sovereignty. Let God be God.

It's Not God's Will for Everyone to Be Healed

This brings us to our fifth and final foundational fact. Simply put, it isn't God's will that everyone be healed in this life. I know that's a hard truth. You'll rarely hear it in contemporary churches. You'll never hear it from health-and-wealth, prosperity-gospel preachers. But the fact is, God never promises that everyone can be healed physically on this side of eternity.

But wait! What about Isaiah 53:5? some would ask. This prophecy of Messiah's suffering for us says, "He was pierced for our rebellion, crushed for our sins. He was beaten so we could be whole. He was whipped so we could be healed." Doesn't that mean Christ's physical suffering assures us of physical healing? Shouldn't every believer cash in on that promise of wholeness and health?

CONSIDER THE CONTEXT

Hold on. We need to consider the context of the verse. Isaiah goes on to say, "All of us, like sheep, have strayed away. We have left God's paths to follow our own. Yet the LORD laid on him the sins of us all" (53:6). He's referring to our sinfulness, not our physical infirmities. In order to deal with our sinful condition, the Lord sent His Son to pay the penalty.

Now look back at verse 5: He was pierced for our *rebellion* and our *sins*. That's the root of our problem. The solution? He was beaten to make us whole, whipped so you and I can be healed. Healed of what? Of our rebellion and sins.

The context of Isaiah 53 is our spiritual sin-sickness, not our physical ailments. All who believe in Jesus experience *spiritual* healing—the complete pardon and forgiveness of all our sins (see Romans 8:1). If Christ had taken on Himself all of our *physical* sicknesses, then everyone who believed in Him would experience instant physical healing. This is far from the case. In my lifetime of ministry, I can count on one hand the number of bona fide, miraculous physical healings I've encountered, and I would have a finger or two left over. Such miracles are very rare. But consider the context, and give thanks to God for His gracious healing of our souls.

CONSIDER THE BIBLICAL EXAMPLES

When we consider examples of sickness in Scripture, it becomes even more clear that it isn't God's will for everyone to be healed in this life. The New Testament puts an end to the popular opinion that God promises physical healing to those who have enough faith. Or to those who confess they're healed against all evidence to the contrary. Or to those who offer up enough "seed money" to the right faith healer. Consider the following biblical examples of prolonged infirmities left unhealed.

Epaphroditus, Paul's "true brother, co-worker, and fellow soldier," almost died because of his illness (Philippians 2:25, 27). He did not experience an instantaneous healing, but God had mercy on him by eventually allowing him to recover (see verse 27). If Paul had the authority to heal the sick at will, Epaphroditus would never have declined to the brink of death. And if miraculous healing had been available for anybody with enough faith, surely Epaphroditus, the "true brother . . . and fellow soldier," would have had at least the faith of a mustard seed needed to move the mountain of sickness from his life!

Later, Paul mentions that he left another colleague, Trophimus, "sick at Miletus" (2 Timothy 4:20). God hadn't healed him yet. Surely, if Christ's sufferings made healing available to every believer, Trophimus wouldn't have been stuck in Miletus because of illness. And if faith healing were a real factor, the apostle Paul, who throughout his ministry performed many "signs and wonders" (2 Corinthians 12:12), would certainly have healed Trophimus.

We need to include Paul's faithful companion Timothy in the list of ministry workers who experienced chronic sickness rather than miraculous healing. In 1 Timothy 5:23, Paul advised his protégé to "drink a little wine for the sake of your stomach because you are sick so often." In those days, people used wine as medicine to help with stomach or digestive problems.[1] We never read of Timothy's chronic sickness being healed by supernatural means. Rather, it appears that Timothy had to treat his frequent illnesses throughout his life.

Finally, we have the example of the apostle Paul himself. Shortly after his conversion, he had been instantly healed of blindness (see Acts 9:17-18). And during his ministry, God healed people in astonishing ways (see Acts 14:9-10; 19:11-12; 28:8). Yet in 2 Corinthians 12, Paul mentions the "thorn" in his flesh that God used to keep him humble (verse 7). We can't know for sure what this condition entailed. We know it involved physical effects, because it was in his "flesh." Many believe it related to failing eyesight. (We'll take a closer look at Paul's experience in chapter 8.)

In any case, so severe was the sting of this "thorn" that Paul pleaded with the Lord three times to take it away (12:8). But each time, God's answer was the same:

No.

No.

No.

God never healed Paul's chronic condition. As far as we know, Paul died still nursing that thorn in the flesh. He was never healed. Why not? Because it isn't God's will that everyone be healed in this life. Please read that again. And please remember it.

But this brings us back around to the original question. The lingering, nagging question: Why, God?

THE NAGGING QUESTION

When I served on the island of Okinawa, I was a member of the Third Division Marine Corp band. On one occasion, we were invited to play an outdoor concert for a leper colony on the north end of Okinawa. The memory of those seriously afflicted men and women will never leave me.

Our band sat in precise rows, decked out in dress blues, our brass and instruments polished and gleaming. The contrast between us and the audience couldn't have been more dramatic. They sat apart, their limbs wrapped in strips of cloth, some of them oozing. Many tried to hide their misshapen faces with what remained of their arms in a sad attempt to cover their shame.

While we performed, those suffering men and women listened in rapt attention. I could barely play my clarinet due to the sadness that weighed on me, seeing bodies horrifically distorted by the disease we now call Hansen's—in biblical times, called leprosy. It broke my heart to see them feeling so unworthy because of a condition they neither caused nor deserved.

The question nagged me. Why was I blessed with the ability to play music while they could barely applaud by banging their limbs together or tapping their crutches on the ground?

Why?

I would have given almost anything to have the power of healing that day. But for His own reasons, God chooses to heal some or let them get well by natural means or with medicine, while allowing others to continue in their sickness, sometimes for the rest of their lives.

The answer to the question *Why?* rests ultimately with God. We can't tell sick people they'll definitely get well if they have enough faith. Nor should we tell people in wheelchairs to stand up and walk. We need to trust God enough to leave each individual case with Him. Back in 1974, on that jumbo jet from Dallas to LA, my colleagues and I knew better than to march to the back of the plane, lay hands on that dying man, and presumptuously declare that he would be healed in the name of Jesus.

The power of healing rests solely with God. We can ask for healing, but He never promised to answer yes. We can even ask why, but God never promised to answer that question either.

The entire book of Job was written with that question in mind. After Job's friends tried (and failed!) to reason their way through the mystery of God's apparent denial of healing for Job, God's reply underscores His wisdom, power, and greatness. The Almighty never answers their question. On the contrary, He questions their answers.

Paul's rousing words in Romans 11:33 are a good summary of the truth about such questions: "Oh, how great are God's riches and wisdom and knowledge! How impossible it is for us to understand his decisions and his ways!"

WHY GOD ALLOWS SUFFERING

God rarely reveals specific reasons why sickness and suffering leave their mark on our lives. Yet Scripture provides some broad-stroke principles to help us understand the God-designed purposes surrounding our trials. I've personally reviewed these principles over and over again during my own sickness and suffering as well as that of my loved ones. These principles are found in 2 Corinthians, among the most autobiographical of all Paul's writings.

Just a glance at Paul's ministry related in the book of Acts reveals a man intimately familiar with suffering and hardship, as summed up in 2 Corinthians: "We were crushed and overwhelmed beyond our ability to endure" (1:8). In the midst of these excruciating experiences, Paul no doubt wrestled with the same *Why* question that you and I contend with. But instead of lamenting his trials, Paul presents three principles outlining why God sometimes chooses not to bring relief or healing.

Suffering Helps Us Comfort Others

First, Paul writes, "He comforts us in all our troubles so that we can comfort others" (2 Corinthians 1:4). Maybe you have faced cancer,

COVID, a stroke, broken bones, multiple sclerosis, Parkinson's, or migraines. Maybe it's a lost job, a natural disaster, a bankruptcy, or a marital betrayal. God comforts us through all these troubles so our hearts will know how to reach out to others with comfort.

Think about it. Who better to console the one who loses a child than someone who's lost a child? Who better to understand a debilitating sickness than one who has gone through the same? Who better understands a child with special needs than one who has a child with special needs?

My son used to have a little sign on the wall of his office that said, "I've learned never to trust the words of anyone who has not gone through serious pain in his or her life." Wise words.

Suffering Keeps Us from Trusting in Ourselves

Second, when circumstances bring us to the end of ourselves, we're forced to turn to God—upon whom we should have been depending from the start. How easy for us to shift our trust from Him to something or someone else. We learn how much we need Him when we get desperately sick. We learn what it means to lean fully on the Lord when the bottom drops out of our lives. Sickness develops a full dependence on Him when our hearts are ready to receive it.

Note how Paul puts it: "We thought we would never live through it. In fact, we expected to die. But as a result, we stopped relying on ourselves and learned to rely only on God, who raises the dead" (2 Corinthians 1:9). If God can raise the dead, He can get you through your suffering and sickness, trials and tragedies.

Even when we succumb to death, we know that He has sealed us with a promise not only of heaven after death but of a glorious bodily resurrection at the return of Christ (see 2 Corinthians 5:1-10).

Suffering Teaches Us to Give Thanks in Everything

Third, as God sees us through the suffering, we learn that bitterness isn't the answer. We learn that complaining doesn't help. We learn, instead, to give thanks to God for the good days. We thank Him for the little blessings, the promises, the hope of the world to come. Reflecting on the effects of God's strengthening grace, Paul wrote, "Then many people will give thanks because God has graciously answered so many prayers for our safety" (2 Corinthians 1:11).

I know thankfulness seems almost inconceivable from a natural point of view. But when God is working in us, we can pray, "Thank You, Lord, that even through this suffering You have some purpose beyond my comprehension. You care for me like I never realized before. Thank You for being to me what no one else can ever be. Thank You that sadness may come through the night, but joy comes in the morning. Thank You for Your relief. Thank You for sustaining me. Thank You that I can be a testimony of Your preserving grace."

UNANSWERED QUESTIONS . . .

I hope I've made it clear that it's not God's will to heal everyone. God has His reasons for healing some and not healing others. In this chapter we focused mostly on why God allows us to continue in our suffering and sickness and lets suffering make its mark in our lives. In the next chapter, we'll explore the other side of this issue—when God heals body and soul.

Regardless of how God chooses to work in our lives, we can trust His goodness and wisdom. Even in the midst of suffering.

Let me close this chapter with some moving words from Philip Yancey's magnificent book, *Where Is God When It Hurts?*

Where is God when it hurts?

He has been there from the beginning. . . .

He transforms pain, using it to teach and strengthen us, if we allow it to turn us toward him. . . .

He lets us cry out, like Job, in loud fits of anger against him, blaming him for a world we spoiled.

He allies himself with the poor and suffering, founding a kingdom tilted in their favor. He stoops to conquer.

He promises supernatural help to nourish the spirit, even if our physical suffering goes unrelieved.

He has joined us. He has hurt and bled and cried and suffered. He has dignified for all time those who suffer, by sharing their pain.

He is with us now, ministering to us through his Spirit and through members of his body who are commissioned to bear us up and relieve our suffering for the sake of the head.

He is waiting, gathering the armies of good. One day he will unleash them, and the world will see one last terrifying moment of suffering before the full victory is ushered in. Then, God will create for us a new, incredible world. And pain shall be no more.[2]

When the questions come and the suffering seems too much to bear, cling to the truth that God has a loving purpose in it. He understands your struggles, and He is there with you in the midst of them, providing strength to endure. Look to Him with a thankful heart, and He will see you through!

CHAPTER 3

WHEN GOD HEALS BODY AND SOUL

Wisdom When Sin Is Causing Your Pain

DURING AN OUTBREAK OF THE BUBONIC PLAGUE nearly five hundred years ago, the no-nonsense leader of the German Reformation, Martin Luther, wrote a practical letter of advice to Johann Hess, a pastor in the city of Breslau. Many of his words relating to Christians' response to sickness have stood the test of time. To those who "tempted God" by recklessly rejecting available measures to counteract the disease, Luther wrote:

> They disdain the use of medicines; they do not avoid places and persons infected by the plague, but lightheartedly make sport of it and wish to prove how independent they are. They say that it is God's punishment; if he wants to protect them he can do so without medicines or our carefulness.

This is not trusting God but tempting him. God has created medicines and provided us with intelligence to guard and take good care of the body so that we can live in good health.[1]

In contrast to such brash folly masked as bold faith, Luther counseled:

I shall ask God mercifully to protect us. Then I shall fumigate, help purify the air, administer medicine, and take it. I shall avoid places and persons where my presence is not needed in order not to become contaminated and thus perchance infect and pollute others, and so cause their death as a result of my negligence. If God should wish to take me, he will surely find me and I have done what he has expected of me and so I am not responsible for either my own death or the death of others. If my neighbor needs me, however, I shall not avoid place or person but will go freely, as stated above.[2]

Those words are as relevant in the twenty-first century as they were in the sixteenth. We have wrestled with these matters of sickness, plague, death, faith, healing, and medicine since the fall of humanity, when sin and suffering intruded on a good creation (see Genesis 3).

In the previous chapter, we asked some difficult questions about sin, sickness, and why God would allow us to suffer in this life. We underscored the important biblical truth that—contrary to the distorted theology of faith healers—it is not God's will that everyone who is suffering or sick be healed in this life.

I view that last chapter like the underside of a rug—it is the biblical theology weaving together our understanding of sin, suffering, and sickness. In this chapter, we flip the rug over and examine the other side of the issue: when God heals body and soul. When we're finished with this examination, we won't have the answers to every question that nags us, but we'll be a few steps closer to a more balanced, biblical way of looking at sin, suffering, and sickness.

SPECIAL GRACE AND COMMON GRACE

Some questions about healing are easy to answer. "Can God heal?" Yes, of course. He can do anything, and the Bible testifies to many miraculous healings. "Yeah, but can God heal in the twenty-first century?" Absolutely. He can and does. In fact, every time you recover from an illness, you've experienced healing. Every time a physician diagnoses a disease and prescribes a successful treatment, you've been healed.

I know what you're thinking: *That's not God healing. That's nature doing its thing.* Now's a good time to introduce a couple of important categories to help us better understand how God heals: *special grace* and *common grace.*

Special grace refers to God's special work in the lives of some people, at specific times. Special grace includes salvation, the indwelling of the Spirit, and other unique special blessings. It can also describe miracles like the deliverance of Israel out of Egypt or the supernatural healing of a man born blind. Only by God's sovereign will does anybody receive the blessings of special grace.

On the other hand, common grace refers to "grace extended to all persons through God's general providence; for example, his provision of sunshine and rain for everyone."[3] We see common grace through the acts of God's goodness, mercy, and love woven into the very fabric of creation itself. That includes God's generous provision of natural remedies for sickness, scientific discoveries resulting in medicines, and the body's own healing power and intricate immune system for fighting infections. All of these come from God's common grace—His fatherly care for all.

Every time you recover from a sickness, every time a vaccine wards off an infection, every time a broken bone heals, you're experiencing God's grace. These healings may not be miracles, which are manifestations of God's special grace, but they're still demonstrations of His goodness and mercy toward you.

Let me be clear. It's not that sometimes God heals by supernatural miracles but other times nature heals us apart from God's power. Whenever we're healed, we're healed by God's power. Period. Yes, sometimes God heals through miracles, but most of the time He heals through a strong immune system, effective medicine, a skilled physician, or a successful medical procedure.

Remember, God isn't obligated to heal us, either by miracle or by medicine, by special grace or common grace. You may know of cases in which two people received the exact same treatment for a disease, but only one recovered. Nobody is healed apart from the grace of God.

MISCONCEPTIONS ABOUT HEALING

Confusing common grace and special grace is one error people make when it comes to healing. But when you or somebody you love is struggling with sickness, you'll hear a lot of bad theology about healing.

For example, some will say you're not getting better because you have hidden sin in your life. So, if you repent and confess your sin, your sickness will go away. But sometimes they will say the sin is a secret even to you! Maybe you need to dig deep down, examine your past, probe your thoughts—but it's there—somewhere. Be careful! We saw in chapter 2 that in those instances when a direct relationship exists between our sin and sickness, the sin and guilt are blatant and apparent. Much of the time, though, there's no relationship between personal sin and sickness.

Other people will say you're sick because you don't have enough faith. If you'll just believe God for the healing and trust in His promises, they say, you'll get what you ask for. But if that were true, why are so few actually healed? Why are real, miraculous healings so rare? Why do most testimonies of supernatural healing turn out to be bogus rumors, hearsay, or flimsy fibs? Is faith the size of a mustard seed that rare?

Still others will try to persuade you to plant "seed money" in the pocket of some faith healer to reap a harvest of health. Then, they claim, you'll receive the healing touch from someone "anointed" with the power of signs, wonders, and miracles. Well, countless charlatans claim to have power that not even the New Testament apostles had—and you'll recognize them by their lack of fruit.

No, none of these claims mesh with Scripture. Those twisted teachings don't help people struggling with sickness. They don't strengthen faith. Instead, they frustrate people, driving them to disillusionment and disappointment with God.

A REAL-LIFE EXAMPLE

As a teenager, Joni Eareckson took a dive off a barge in the Chesapeake Bay, struck bottom, and broke her neck. As a result, she is now bound to a wheelchair, unable to move her legs, and has very limited mobility of her arms. Yet in her long, hard road of handling her disability with tremendous faith, she's had to deal with numerous well-meaning people peddling lies about healing.

In her book *A Place of Healing*, she recounts how one young man named David stopped her after a Sunday morning church service and wanted to pray for her healing. He wasn't the first—Joni often tells of individuals who believed they had been sent by the Holy Spirit to raise her up from her wheelchair. But this young man's approach stood out to her. Joni writes:

> This guy wasted no time in getting down to business, launching into what sounded like a prepared speech. "Have you ever considered that it might be sin standing in the way of your healing? That you've disobeyed in some way?" Before I could answer, David flipped open his Bible . . . and reminded me that the paralyzed man [of Luke 5:18-19] in the story was healed. And I could be, too, if only I would but confess my sins and have faith to believe. He added, "Joni, there *must* be some sin in your life that you haven't dealt with yet."[4]

When Joni insisted she had a clear conscience before God, David eyed her with skepticism. That young man—like countless others—had been taught that for believers, health and wellness are the norm.

Sickness comes only from a lack of faith or an excess of sin. Joni sums up these common misconceptions well:

> According to what [David] had been taught, if I was a Christian, and if there was no known sin in my life, and if I had faith that God could heal, well, then . . . *I would be healed.* Didn't God want everyone healed? Didn't Jesus want everyone well? Of course He did! It was so obvious!
>
> "Joni, you must have a lack of faith. I mean, look at you. You're still in your wheelchair!"[5]

Nobody would want to be out of that wheelchair more than Joni. But it wasn't God's plan for her. She came to terms with that decades ago—and since then, God has used her to minister to countless other people with disabilities around the world.

I have great respect for people who trust God to heal them—whether through common grace or special grace. But I have enormous admiration for people like Joni Eareckson Tada, who steadfastly trust God even when He *doesn't* heal.

BIBLICAL INSTRUCTIONS TO FOLLOW IN SICKNESS

Inspiring stories are great, and bad examples can teach us a lot, but ultimately we need to discover what God says on the matter of healing. Some foundational questions are answered in James 5:13-16. In those few verses, James includes three principles in question-and-answer format. Taken together, these statements help us think biblically about when God heals—body and soul.

When You're Suffering

Look at James's first question: "Are any of you suffering hardships?" (James 5:13). The Greek word translated by the NLT as "suffering hardships" encompasses a broad range of troubles. The word even sounds bad: *kakopatheō*. Though it can include physical illness, we should picture afflictions that are mental, emotional, or spiritual in nature. This would include the kinds of anxiety, doubt, and discouragement brought on by persecution, relationship conflicts, financial hardships, or other similar painful intrusions. Think of external circumstances that cause you inner turmoil. That's *kakopatheō*.

When we suffer such hardships, what do we do? James answers his own question: "You should pray" (5:13).

Pray. Period.

Pray for endurance. Pray for insight. Pray for encouragement. Pray for God to intercede. Pray that He'll build bridges to reconciliation, or that He'll provide for your needs. Pray that He'll replace doubt and anxiety with confidence and peace. Pray!

This reminds me of something I saw on TV back in 1980, shortly after Mount Saint Helens in Washington state literally blew its top. The guy being interviewed was a reporter who had made it back down the mountain alive after a very close call. He had video and a soundtrack of his own life-or-death crisis. He was near the mouth of the volcano when it erupted, and he ran for his life, camera rolling, mic on. Though the pictures were blurred and dark, you could hear the man's voice loud and clear.

He breathed heavily, sobbed, panted—and spoke directly to

God. They say there are no atheists in foxholes. We can be certain there are no atheists on the slopes of an erupting volcano either! His prayer—that's what it was—burst as freely from the depths of his heart as the eruption burst from the mountain behind him. No formality, no clichés—just the despairing cry of a creature deep in trouble. I heard cries like "Oh, God, oh, my God—help! Help!" Panicked, rapid breathing, spitting, gagging, coughing, panting. "It's so hot, so dark! Help me, God! Please, please, please, please, help me!"

That's the kind of prayer that flows from the depths of *kakopatheō*.

In the depths of your own crisis, don't hold back. Bombard God's throne with your pleading. The release of anxiety through prayer helps to heal the soul. I can't explain how that works. I just know it does.

When You're Cheerful

Now for James's second question: "Are any of you happy?" (5:13). Remember everything we said about the emotional pain that comes from suffering hardship? This is the opposite. Instead of anxiety—peace. Instead of turmoil—calm. Instead of sadness—cheerfulness. Instead of affliction—joy.

James knows life is a mixed bag. Yes, we sometimes endure long autumns of loss or prolonged winters of suffering. But other times God brings us through seasons of springtime, when everything comes to life again, or fruitful summers of bountiful blessing. What do we do when we experience those seasons of joy?

Some people forget about God in the good times. They are quick to blame Him when things go wrong, but they ignore Him when things go well.

Or they treat Him like a 911 operator, crying out to Him only in emergencies.

James has a better answer: "You should sing praises" (5:13). The Greek word used here for singing, *psallō*, originally referred to playing a stringed instrument. You probably notice the similarity between *psallō* and our English word *psalm*. The word pictures a heart filled with praises, songs of joy, celebration, exuberant delight. In other words, when you're so cheerful that you're ready to burst, let it out! As much as you would bombard heaven with your prayers for help when suffering, belt out praises toward heaven with songs of celebration when you are feeling happy.

Now, let's be real. Sometimes our days are bright and sunny, sometimes dark and stormy. But most of the time each day has some of each—it's partly cloudy. It starts out cheerful and ends with a crisis. Or the rain keeps falling while God paints a rainbow across the gloomy sky. Our days don't roll out in black or white. Most often they linger in the gray. That's all the more reason to sing His praises for those beams of light that pierce the clouds.

Joyous praise and thanksgiving are like a balm for the soul.

So, let there be praise!

When You're Sick

James's third question is a little more complicated. Its answer requires three verses. He asks, "Are any of you sick?" (5:14). The Greek word for sick, *astheneō*, can also be translated "weak" or "feeble." It can refer to people who are "weak in faith" (see Romans 4:19; 14:1) as well as to those weakened by physical illness (see Luke 4:40; Acts 9:37).

These people are incapacitated, maybe even bedridden. Besides diseases or injuries, we can think of other conditions that sideline us. Perhaps you have dealt with depression, exhaustion, stress, or even extreme guilt. Whatever the issue, you just can't go on. You're like a derelict vehicle on the side of the road: you've broken down or run out of gas.

So, what do you do? James offers three clear steps for us when we are facing serious illness.

TAKE THE INITIATIVE

First, James tells us, the sick person must "call for the elders of the church" (5:14). I know from personal experience that pastors are often the last to know when somebody in the church is sick, hospitalized, or incapacitated. In fact, those who are sick sometimes don't want anybody to know it. This is true especially of private or proud people. Resist that approach! The body of Christ is a family. We're called to care for one another, to bear one another's burdens. So, share your suffering with others. Don't keep it a secret!

INFORM YOUR CHURCH LEADERS

James next mentions a specific response by the leaders of the church: "to come and pray over you, anointing you with oil in the name of the Lord" (5:14). These two actions—prayer and anointing—occur together. What is this anointing? We find two primary uses of oil in Scripture: ceremonial and medicinal. As an example of the first category, think of Samuel consecrating young David as king of Israel in a solemn ceremonial act (1 Samuel 16:13). In the second category, recall the Samaritan pouring wine and oil on the wounds of the injured man on the side of the road (Luke 10:34). The wine cleansed the wounds, while the oil soothed them and protected the man from infection.

The Greek word James uses for "anointing," *aleiphō*, points to the second use of oil. By offering prayer *and* anointing with medicinal or soothing oil, the leaders of the church attend to both soul and body. The Bible presents no contradiction between praying and using medicine. In fact, we use medicine with thankfulness and prayerfulness, because even these "natural" treatments have come to us by God's common grace.

Let me apply this to our day. When church leaders come to pray for the sick, their first questions should include "Have you been to a doctor? Are you taking your medicine?" In the ancient world, medicine was still a fairly primitive science. Various oils certainly helped many kinds of ailments, but treatments have come a long way in the last two thousand years. Had James been writing to twenty-first-century readers, he would no doubt have advised, "In the name of the Lord, pray over the sick and give them their medicine." Medicine shouldn't be our last resort. Nor should prayer. These healing agents work together.

LEAVE THE RESULTS TO GOD

Finally, we must remember that if it's God's will, He will ultimately provide the healing—not the oil, not the medicine, not the physicians, not the elders, not even the prayer itself. Praying in the name of the Lord (see John 14:14) always means praying according to *His* will, not ours. Then we must leave the results to Him.

What If God Doesn't Heal?

In the kind of case James has in mind, he presents the specific results of the elders' prayer and anointing offered in faith: restoration, raising up, and forgiveness. The NASB says, "The prayer of faith will restore the one who is sick, and the Lord will raise him up" (James 5:15). At first glance, this seems to suggest that as long as the elders do their part—pray and anoint—then God will grant healing, every time.

But wait.

What happens when it doesn't work?

The elders of the church where I've served as pastor for many years have followed James's prescription faithfully on numerous occasions. Sometimes the people for whom they've prayed recover. Sometimes, though, the individual dies. Is that the fault of the elders? A lack of faith? The wrong kind of "oil"? No. As we saw in the previous chapter, it isn't always the Father's will that a person be healed. The New Testament provides many examples in which God's answer to a "prayer of faith" was no.

The context of James's instruction helps to clear up the confusion. Remember, as we also saw in the previous chapter, that sometimes our mental and emotional weariness, physical suffering, and sickness can be caused by our personal sins. Notice the third result of the "prayer of faith" offered by the elders: "and if he has committed sins, they will be forgiven him." The very next verse underscores this idea: "Confess your sins to each other and pray for each other so that you may be healed" (5:16). This context suggests that James had in mind situations in which sickness came as a result of sin.

Though not all cases of physical illness are the result of sin, sometimes this is the case. If so, no amount of medicinal oil can treat that spiritual wound. It takes a balm of repentance, confession, and restoration to heal the soul. This seems to be what James had in mind. If a person's sickness is a result of personal sin, they will be restored, raised up, and forgiven—healed in both body and soul. But remember, not all sickness is connected to personal sin.

A TRUE HEALING OF BODY AND SOUL

Years ago, I was asked to join a small group of elders to pray for an ill woman, bedridden in an ICU. I didn't know the woman well. Her husband was a physician and was one of the elders in the group. She had been receiving the best medical care available at the time, but her condition hadn't improved. Many were concerned for her life.

When we walked into that room, she could hardly move her limbs. She barely blinked, as if she were in a daze or sedated. Her dull complexion made it seem that death was near. Even from my limited perspective, her situation didn't look good. I glanced at her physician husband and saw fear and desperation in his eyes.

In obedience to James 5, we began to pray. Tears fell, voices cracked. We cast all our hopes on God to work, to bring relief, to bring comfort, and, if it be His will, to bring healing. I'll never forget how our words flowed with passionate sincerity. One man prayed, then another picked up where he left off. I prayed for her, then when another began, the woman's weak voice interrupted us: "Stop. Stop right here. Stop!"

We all grew silent and looked into her face. She began to blink, as if she were coming out of a mental fog. She took a deep breath. "I . . . I have some things to tell you all." To our surprise, out of her mouth poured an earnest confession of her life of hidden sin. It came as a complete shock to her husband. He knew none of it. Moved to compassion and forgiveness, he reached over to embrace her. "Wait," she said. And before all of us—some of whom were total strangers— she continued to confess moral failures, unfaithfulness, lies, a life of ongoing hypocrisy.

I can't explain it, but as she confessed her sins, the color came back into her face. As she unloaded her burden, some of her strength seemed to return. She sobbed as she poured out her confession.

When she finished, I don't think there was a dry eye in the room. Our hearts went out to her and her husband. We stepped back as he stepped closer, then we quietly left the room as husband and wife wept tears of brokenness and reconciliation. Her confession of personal sins brought the relief of forgiveness. And with that came restoration and healing.

In a short time, she was transferred from the ICU. Within days she was walking the halls of the hospital on a straight path to recovery. Within the week she was home again, regaining her strength. It was clear that God had done a miracle there. He had marvelously healed that woman—body and soul. He also restored their marriage.

Through that experience, I believe I witnessed firsthand the kind of situation James had in mind.

REFRAMING OUR SUFFERING

A few years back, our daughter Colleen launched a new and effective ministry at Insight for Living: "Reframing Ministries." The name refers to the ways God reframes our lives as a result of great suffering, loss, disability, hardship, or tragedy. She tells her own story in *Reframing Life: Focusing on God When Life Gets Sideways.*[6] Through the ministry, she's been able to turn her struggles into opportunities to encourage and empower others dealing with life's disorienting circumstances. She learned that even if God doesn't take the pain away, He'll use it to change us. To refashion our character. To refocus our priorities. To renew our purpose.

With that in mind, let me leave you with four practical principles that will help you "reframe" your perspective when facing questions of suffering, sickness, and God's healing touch. In light of what we've discovered about how God heals, I think these principles will escort us in new directions on life's journey, especially along those inevitable bumpy roads. They revolve around four key terms: *confess, pray, seek,* and *thank.*

1. **Confess your sins.** Let me repeat that not all sickness relates to our personal sins. I'm not saying you always need to dissect your heart, mind, and motives, trying to find some unconscious sin that may be the root of your problems. My point is that self-examination, honesty, repentance, and reconciliation with others always contributes to spiritual healing and health. Confession turns the focus from the physical ailments to the spiritual condition, where true wholeness must begin.

So, confess your sins. We tend to hold back, double down on excuses, or deny wrongdoing. Don't hide your sin. And never withhold reconciliation from those you've sinned against. Seek resolution with whomever you have offended.

2. **Pray for each other.** Like confession, prayer also provides healing to the soul. Pray when you wake up in the morning, pray when your head hits the pillow at night, and pray throughout the day. Bring everything to the Lord. Pray for others. Ask how you can pray for them. Follow up later to see how God has responded to those prayers. James says, "The earnest prayer of a righteous person has great power and produces wonderful results" (James 5:16).

Yes, pray for those who are sick. Bring your physical concerns to God. He invites that. He wants to hear from you. But also pray for those spiritual attributes that will help you walk through the suffering—"love, joy, peace, patience, kindness, goodness, faithfulness, gentleness, and self-control" (Galatians 5:22-23).

3. **Seek medical treatment when needed.** By His common grace, God filled this world with countless remedies and treatments that have been discovered over the millennia. He also gave us reason, wisdom, and problem-solving abilities to make use of these things. As a result, most of us have access to medical care and physicians with specialized training and experience. In light of all this, I find it hard to pray for anyone who refuses medical attention. God wants us to avail ourselves of these provisions.

I like how the Reformer John Calvin, put it: "If we

reflect that the Spirit of God is the only fountain of truth, we will be careful . . . not to reject or condemn truth wherever it appears. In despising the gifts, we insult the Giver."[7] The truths gained by medical science are gifts we should receive with thanksgiving.

4. **When healing comes from God, thank Him for it.** Receive God's blessing with thankfulness and praise. God can heal us of anything, anytime, anywhere—by any method He chooses. It's all in His sovereign hands.

   When He chooses *not* to heal—or at least not to heal *immediately*—He doesn't owe us an explanation. He's the Potter; we're the clay. He's the Master; we're the servants. He's God; we're not. Continue to seek Him, to serve Him, and to trust Him. And in those moments when God chooses to grant you health, return praises to Him, knowing that "whatever is good and perfect is a gift coming down to us from God our Father" (James 1:17).

I've said several times in the last two chapters that it's not God's will for everyone who is suffering or sick to be healed *in this life*. Those last three words are important. They anticipate a future when all believers will be raised in glorious resurrection bodies to live eternally with their Creator in a new heaven and a new earth. I cling to that promise with hope and longing. One day—perhaps today—the Lord will ultimately answer centuries of prayers for healing with a complete banishment of sin, sickness, suffering, and death. Hear these words from the throne of God, and rejoice in them: "Look, God's home is now among his people! He will live with them, and they will be his people. God himself will be with them. He will wipe every tear from their eyes, and there will be no more death or sorrow or crying or pain. All these things are gone forever" (Revelation 21:3-4).

What a magnificent promise to claim!

CHAPTER 4

WHEN UNEXPECTED TESTS RATTLE OUR WORLD

Wisdom When God Is Testing Your Faith

BACK IN 1940, as the Nazi Luftwaffe began its blitz bombings of England, no one could have predicted how merciless the attacks would become. The air raids continued for eight full months. With London as their frequent target, Hitler and his brutal associates hoped to bring the prime minister, Winston Churchill, to his knees. Obviously, they didn't know Churchill. People didn't call him the "British Bulldog" for nothing.

In November of that year, Churchill made this powerful statement in a speech to the House of Commons: "It is not given to human beings, happily for them, . . . to foresee or to predict to any large extent the unfolding course of events."[1]

More often than not, wise living means learning to roll with the punches.

Though we often wish we could peer around the corner of life's twisting path to foresee or predict every trial, test, and tribulation, God has mercifully spared us from this. I say spared us because if we knew beforehand every hardship we would face, we'd be in a constant state of preemptive panic and on-edge anxiety. If you really think about it, none of us would want that.

Consider Solomon's wise words: "Don't brag about tomorrow, since you don't know what the day will bring" (Proverbs 27:1). And Jesus said, "Don't worry about tomorrow, for tomorrow will bring its own worries. Today's trouble is enough for today" (Matthew 6:34). The Bible is clear: we should neither boast nor fret over tomorrow, because we can never know what's lurking just around the corner. No wonder James warns pretentious planners to temper their over-confident business ventures with healthy humility: "How do you know what your life will be like tomorrow? Your life is like the morning fog—it's here a little while, then it's gone. What you ought to say is, 'If the Lord wants us to, we will live and do this or that'" (James 4:14-15).

FINDING HOPE IN GOD'S WORD

I've had some grueling trials in my life—and so have you. Though we may look back on our less painful experiences with a nervous chuckle or even a sunny sigh of relief, there's nothing funny or frivolous about God's testing. Even though we know better in our head, in our heart it sometimes feels like He's pushing us not just to the edge of the cliff but over the edge—and delighting in it! How easy it is to release our grip on God's goodness, sovereignty, and wisdom in those moments.

Yet just when we think it's "lights out" for us, God breaks through the silence and says, as it were, "I'm right here with you. I've never left you. I know you trust Me. You've passed the test!" In those moments we learn without a doubt that the Sunday-school God of goodness, sovereignty, and wisdom is the same God who shows up on those long, dark Mondays that assault our peace of mind and put our theology to the test.

When trials happen—and they will—we turn to Scripture for encouragement through accounts of other big tests nobody expected. We need to be reassured by examples of God using life-altering, hope-challenging, faith-stretching episodes to test and shape His people.

We don't have to look hard to find them.

In the pages of His Word, we see God at work in the unexpected tests that rattle our world. Through them, He brings change to our lives. These trials may feel like pointless detours from God's perfect plan or like absolute disasters from which we'll never recover. But they are neither.

God is always working out His perfect will behind the scenes. Pain and heartache often accompany those tests and trials, but in the end, something good invariably comes about for those who endure by God's life-giving grace.

God doesn't give us a warning before the test. But we can be confident that He will provide what we need in the midst of it. And He will accomplish His purposes through it.

I can think of no better biblical example of an unexpected test than the one recorded in Genesis 22. In this story, Abraham had his world rattled by an experience he could never have anticipated. If you could have sat down with Abraham the day before and asked him to imagine the most bizarre and seemingly irrational trial God could throw his way, this one would have beaten anything he could have come up with.

TWO TYPES OF TESTS

Before launching into the story of Abraham, let's consider two types of tests through which God brings His people. Let's call them "sudden bursts" and "slow burns." Like an explosion, the sudden burst breaks into our lives instantly. It flares up hot and bright for a brief season—maybe a few days or weeks—then just as suddenly becomes part of our past. The effects may linger like smoldering embers, but the direct pain and stress of the test passes away, and our life returns to normal. I'm sure you've experienced such sudden bursts—a quick bout of the flu, a broken bone, a marriage crisis, a financial blow, or a minor car accident.

The other kind of test is the slow burn. It may not be as intense as the sudden burst, but what it lacks in severity it makes up in duration. For months, years, and even decades, it greets us every morning and tucks us in at night. You know the kinds of struggles I'm talking about—chronic pain with no prospects for a cure, lifelong strained relationships with family members, a wayward teenager, long-term depression constantly holding us back and dragging us down.

When I was just a boy, the Swindolls occasionally enjoyed a family reunion at my grandfather's bay cottage near the Gulf in south Texas. Because the crowd was so large, we'd hire a man named Coats to help with the cooking. I'll never forget him. Not just his cooking, but his quaint comments are a lasting memory for me.

I remember standing near Coats one evening at sunset, watching him smear sauce on the meat slow-cooking over the coals. He was telling me about his life, which had been marked by numerous troubles and tragedies—some sudden bursts, some slow burns. At one point Coats knelt down to my level, looked in my eyes, and said: "Little Charles—the hardest thing about life is that it's so *daily*."

So daily! What a simple but profound way of describing both the sudden bursts and slow burns of difficulty that God allows in our lives. The tests that come like a flash and last no longer than a dash seldom do more than bring a brief crash. On the other hand, the marathons—the relentless, incessant, steady, persistent, continual trials that won't go away—they may bruise us, but they build character.

But sometimes—as in the case of Abraham—the test is a sudden burst with such intensity that its memory and effects never go away. It's more like an atom bomb than a hand grenade. This brief episode—just nineteen verses of the Bible—is God's final exam for Abraham, who had endured numerous tests of his faith throughout his life.

And this one hits him where it hurts the most.

A TEST ONE HUNDRED YEARS IN THE MAKING

Don't lose sight of the backdrop for this episode in Genesis 22. In the previous chapter, God had graciously fulfilled His promise to Abraham and his wife, Sarah, that He would bless them with a son of their own (see Genesis 15:4; 17:19; 18:10). It was to be through this son that future generations of Hebrews as well as all the nations of the earth would be blessed (18:18).

After long, agonizing, doubt-filled years of waiting and waiting and waiting some more—Isaac is born (see Genesis 21:2)! The name Isaac comes from a Hebrew word for "laughter"—memorializing forever the reactions of Abraham and Sarah at the thought of having a newborn baby at the ages of one hundred and ninety, respectively (see Genesis 17:17; 18:12). But this child of promise is no laughing matter. Future generations, countless descendants, and worldwide—even *eternal*—blessings are riding on him.

The intense bond of love between father and son can't be put into words. It isn't just an old man loving a little baby. When Abraham cradles that fragile newborn in his arms, holds that toddler's hands, teaches that adolescent the facts of life, mentors that teen in what it means to be a man—all these are investments in a glorious future that would bless even the nations!

Yet, when we turn the page from the birth of Isaac in Genesis 21 to the unexpected events of chapter 22, the tone changes from lingering delight to sudden dismay. The story jumps ahead at least fifteen years. When the scene opens, Isaac is probably in his midteens or so. Not an infant, not a toddler, not even a preteen. That young man is strong enough to haul a stack of wood on his shoulders (see Genesis 22:6). This would make Isaac between fifteen and twenty years old; Abraham would be pushing 120.

For the previous century, Abraham had experienced numerous tests of his faith and obedience. He had to rely on God when he left his native country and set out for a land that God would show him (see Genesis 12:1). He had to trust in God's protection during days of conflict and crisis with Lot (see chapter 14). He had to believe God and let go of his own reason and desires when God insisted the promise would come through his own child rather than through Ishmael (see chapters 16–17). He had to lean into God's goodness in the days of judgment on Sodom and Gomorrah (see chapters 18–19). Through that long century of trials and tests, God reminded Abraham again and again that He would give him a son. And through those decades, Abraham's faith grew.

Yahweh—the one true God—was good.

Yahweh—the one true God—could be trusted.

Then, out of the blue, an unexpected trial rattles Abraham's world and puts everything he believes about Yahweh to the test.

ABRAHAM'S FINAL EXAM

We are told right up front, "Some time later, God tested Abraham's faith" (Genesis 22:1). Abraham won't know until the end that it is a test. All Abraham knows is what God commands completely out of the blue: "Take your son, your only son—yes, Isaac, whom you love so much—and go to the land of Moriah. Go and sacrifice him as a burnt offering on one of the mountains, which I will show you" (22:2).

We might call this a final comprehensive exam—the climax of Abraham's life of faith and obedience. Abraham's journey of faith was launched with a command to leave the land God would show him; it lands with a command to go to a mountain God would show him. It started with a mandate to let go of his beloved family; it ends with letting go of his beloved son. It began with sacrificing his past; it concludes with sacrificing his future. (See Genesis 12:1-2; 22:1-2.)

In this final exam, God chooses to put Abraham's faith and obedience to the test through an unthinkable, unprecedented, and— one could even argue—*irrational* command. In fact, let's be honest. On the surface of it, God's mandate appears inconsistent with His character—theologically baffling and morally wrong!

Now, let me repeat—*we* know this was a test. God had no intention of letting Isaac die at the hand of his father (see Genesis 22:1). In fact, God intended all along to apply the principle of redeeming a human life with the death of an animal as a substitute for another (see Exodus 34:20). But let me also remind you that Abraham doesn't know any of this. All he has to go by is the straightforward command: *Go and sacrifice your son.*

Before I go further, you must put yourself in the place of Abraham. If you are a parent, this won't be difficult. Perhaps you have lost a son or daughter. I can't imagine an agony that could be worse. But what if God asked you to give them up? It's hard enough walking your child to that first kindergarten class, hugging your son goodbye at the door of his college dorm, or letting go of your daughter's hand after walking her down the aisle on her wedding day. But to send your only son into eternity by your own hand?

Unthinkable!

ABRAHAM'S RESPONSE

None of us could say for sure what we would have done in Abraham's situation. But we know what Abraham did. Three specific aspects stand out about his response: it is immediate, it is based on faith alone, and it shows thorough and complete obedience.

Abraham's Response Is Immediate

Look at the very next words after God's shocking command: "The next morning Abraham got up early" (Genesis 22:3). No middle-of-the-night pleading, arguing, or bargaining. No long, five-course breakfast to give God time to change His mind. Abraham doesn't explain to God how long he and Sarah had waited for the birth of Isaac. No mention of his old age or his past performance in the realms of faith and obedience. No clutching, no clinging, no crying. Instead, he just gets up and goes: "He saddled his donkey and took two of his servants with him, along with his son, Isaac" (22:3).

Abraham's Response Is Based on Faith Alone

The author of Hebrews gives us some important insight here: "It was by faith that Abraham offered Isaac as a sacrifice when God was testing him" (11:17). *By faith!* Think about it. By faith he chops the wood. By faith he takes the three-day journey from Beersheba to Moriah (see Genesis 22:3-4). Then, when he sees the mount from a distance, by faith he tells his servants, "The boy and I will travel a little farther. We will worship there, and then we will come right back" (22:5).

Did you catch that? "*We* will come right back." Not "I"—"*We*."

Hebrews explains: "Abraham, who had received God's promises, was ready to sacrifice his only son, Isaac, even though God had told him, 'Isaac is the son through whom your descendants will be counted'" (11:17-18). Though Abraham doesn't have all the details of *how* God will keep His promises concerning Isaac, he trusts that God *will* keep His promises. In fact, "Abraham reasoned that if Isaac died, God was able to bring him back to life again" (11:19). Abraham never wavers in his confidence in the goodness and wisdom of God. He knows that his God has never done anything wrong, nor could He ever be cruel.

In this final exam, God puts Abraham's faith to the ultimate test. It is, in essence, a single-question, true-false exam that goes something like this:

> True or False: God is completely good, wise, just, and
> powerful, and He can be trusted to do what's right even
> when something unexpected rattles our world.

The purpose of a good exam is not to teach students something they don't know. It's to give them an opportunity to demonstrate what they've learned. In Abraham's exam, the Lord is saying, in effect, "I want your whole heart—total trust and full obedience." When Abraham answers "True" to that profound test of faith, he gives his Lord and God everything he has with complete trust and obedience.

And he gives with total abandon.

Oswald Chambers' description of unreserved faith in his classic work, *My Utmost for His Highest*, fits the faith of Abraham well: "Faith is the heroic effort of your life, you fling yourself in reckless confidence on God."[2] Isn't that great? You rarely see that kind of faith in our over-rationalized, me-centered world. Chambers continues:

> If a man is going to do anything worth while, there are
> times when he has to risk everything on his leap, and in
> the spiritual domain Jesus Christ demands that you risk
> everything you hold by common sense and leap into what
> He says. . . . Only one out of a crowd is daring enough to
> bank his faith in the character of God.[3]

That's exactly what Abraham does. His response to God's command is immediate—based on faith in the character of God alone.

Returning to the story, we don't want to miss a brief but riveting dialogue between father and son as they walk together. It reveals the depths of Abraham's complete faith in his God:

Isaac turned to Abraham and said, "Father?"

"Yes, my son?" Abraham replied.

"We have the fire and the wood," the boy said, "but where is the sheep for the burnt offering?"

"God will provide a sheep for the burnt offering, my son," Abraham answered. And they both walked on together.

GENESIS 22:7-8

In response to Isaac's question, Abraham places the burden on God to solve this dilemma between his knowledge of the Lord's character and the bizarre nature of His command. The original Hebrew text reads more literally, "God will provide for Himself the lamb" (Genesis 22:8, NASB). The word "will provide" is actually the verb "to see." In other words, God will "see to it" that Abraham has what he needs.

This isn't just wishful thinking on Abraham's part. He isn't trying to deceive Isaac to keep him from running home to tell mom. And I don't think Abraham has some special revelation detailing how God will ultimately "see to it." Rather, Abraham knows that one way or another, God will see to the sacrifice, maintain His character, and keep His promises.

The actual how is left to God alone.

Abraham's Response Shows Thorough and Complete Obedience

The third aspect of Abraham's response flows from the second. Because of his complete faith in God, he obeys thoroughly and completely. When they arrive at the mount, Abraham does just as he had been told: "Abraham built an altar and arranged the wood on it. Then he tied his son, Isaac, and laid him on the altar on top of the wood. And Abraham picked up the knife to kill his son as a sacrifice" (Genesis 22:9-10).

At this point, I'm just as impressed by Isaac's trust in his father as by Abraham's trust in God. On Isaac's part, we see no running, no questions, no resistance, no fight. On Abraham's part, no hesitation, no hemming and hawing, no looking to heaven for reassurance, and no countdown to buy time. With knife raised, Abraham is ready and willing to go through with the act in thorough and complete obedience.

HEAVEN'S PROVISION

Just when Abraham is about to follow through with the command, a familiar voice breaks the silence. Genesis 22:11 says, "At that moment the angel of the LORD called to him from heaven, 'Abraham! Abraham!'" The repetition of his name indicates the urgency. The implication is that without the timely heavenly intervention, Abraham would have carried out the command, just as he understood it. He would have offered his son to God as a burnt offering.

I can imagine that to Abraham's ears the words of the angel seemed like the "Hallelujah Chorus" breaking out in the midst of silence: "'Don't lay a hand on the boy!' the angel said. 'Do not hurt him in any way, for now I know that you truly fear God. You have not withheld from me even your son, your only son'" (Genesis 22:12).

At that moment, Abraham knows it was a test. Isaac is spared. Abraham looks up and sees, stuck by the horns in a nearby thicket, a ram, which he offers as a substitute for his son (Genesis 22:13). God's goodness and wisdom are vindicated, and Abraham passes the final comprehensive exam. He demonstrates the genuineness of his faith, and no question remains as to whom he loves and holds first in his life.

What an unforgettable, unexpected test!

A few years ago, when Cynthia and I were designing the Insight for Living Ministries International Headquarters building, we wanted to find a piece of art that would make a statement about how God had led us to that point. The story of how God grew that local radio program into an international, multilingual ministry is nothing short of phenomenal.

I say this not to boast about us—believe me, I'm just as surprised at what God did as anybody. Through a series of often unexpected and sometimes harrowing tests and trials that rattled our world, the Lord proved faithful beyond our dreams. Yes, we sometimes made missteps and miscalculations along the way. But God provided. At times we underestimated what He would do and planned for less than He had in mind. But God always "saw to it."

I often shake my head and smile at how two undeserving people from two tiny towns in Texas, with no background in radio or media, ended up where we did. We were thrust into this adventure by God's step-by-step direction, which often involved painful lessons in letting go of the worldly supports we were clinging to—whether people, plans, possessions, or positions.

So, as we looked for a piece of art, our minds continually returned to that epochal scene on Mount Moriah—the test that rattled Abraham's world. Eventually we found a magnificent sculpture by Robert Hogan. It portrays the story we've just walked through, and it stands high on its own pedestal in the entryway of our building. The wings of the angel of the Lord spread out while swooping down from heaven. His hand clasps Abraham's right hand, where the sacrificial blade is raised above his head. Isaac lies bound on the altar of stones. The angel's other hand points at a ram caught in a thicket. At the base of the sculpture a small plaque reads, "The Lord Himself will provide."

That's the story of our ministry. It's the story of our lives. And if you look back over the course of your own life, you'll see it's your story too. God Himself has provided. And He will continue to do so. All glory goes to Him for what He's done and will do—in, with, through, and even in spite of us.

JEHOVAH-JIREH, OUR PROVIDER

You may remember the upbeat worship chorus "Jehovah-Jireh."[4] That name and its significance come directly from Genesis 22:14: "Abraham named the place Yahweh-Yireh (which means 'the LORD will provide'). To this day, people still use that name as a proverb: 'On the mountain of the LORD it will be provided.'" By naming that place "Yahweh-Yireh," Abraham guaranteed that the memory of that unexpected test would stand as a memorial to God's provision from generation to generation. The song "Jehovah-Jireh" continues to point back to that timeless trial, just as Robert Hogan's sculpture reminds us of God's timely provision.

The way Abraham aced the ultimate test of his faith and obedience serves as a vital lesson for us when we face our own unexpected tests that shake us to the core. To apply Abraham's experience on Moriah to our own lives, let me share a couple of principles drawn from that pivotal event.

God Never Puts Us through a Test without a Purpose

If you're going through a trial, God has a purpose for it. If you're facing an unexpected test, you can rest on the fact that it's part of God's plan. I've said this several times and I'll say it again, because it's a vital truth of the Christian life that is too easily forgotten.

I've learned over the years that tests and trials are often designed to have us release something we're clutching. Perhaps you are holding tightly right now to a dream, a person, your possessions, a title or position, a place, or an opinion. It's amazing how a well-placed test can loosen us from what we've been gripping with white knuckles.

Shortly before her death, Corrie ten Boom attended our church in Southern California. You may be familiar with her inspiring story of persevering faith as told in her most famous book, *The Hiding Place*. One Sunday following the worship service, I met briefly with her to express our love and respect for her faithful example through the years.

In that conversation, she asked about my family, my children, their names and ages. Detecting my great love for each of them, she cupped her wrinkled hands in front of me and passed on a tender admonishment I'll never forget. I can still recall that strong Dutch accent: "Pastor Svendahl, you must learn to hold everyting loosely. Even your dear family. Why? Because da Fater may vish to take vun of tem back to Himself, und ven He does, it vill hurt you if He must pry your fingers loose."

Having tightened her hands together while saying those words, she slowly opened them and smiled so kindly as she added, "Remember: hold everyting loosely. Everyting."

Since our Lord is sovereign, not only are our times in His hands, but so are all our possessions and all the people we love. Surrendering our rights to Him includes the deliberate releasing of our grip on everything and everyone. Yes, every thing—and every one!

When We Trust God, He Provides Solutions

When we put our trust in God—even when we don't understand what He's doing—He provides solutions that teach us to live with open hands. When we've passed the test, whether it was a "sudden burst" or a "slow burn," we often learn never to tightly clutch people or possessions again. This doesn't mean God removes them from our lives permanently. Usually not. But we learn to hold them loosely. Then, looking back, we discover that the rewards that come with holding things loosely surpass anything we could have otherwise imagined.

Whatever it is you've been gripping, clinging to, trying in every way to hold on to, let it go. When the unexpected test rattles your world, meet it with faith and obedience. You'll be amazed at the surprising ways God steps in. The path and provision He has for you is so much greater than the one you're grasping.

The poet Martha Snell Nicholson, who suffered from debilitating disease most of her life, sums up this principle beautifully in her oft-quoted poem "Treasures." After describing how God seemed to pluck from her hands everything she loved in this world, she portrays a voice from heaven asking her to lift her empty hands to Him, only to receive an abundant outpouring of treasures from heaven. In the final lines of the poem, she concludes, "God could not pour His riches / Into hands already full!"

When Abraham left the scene of his unexpected test and returned home, he loved Isaac just as much as ever, but he never forgot who was meant to have first place in his heart. Maybe you've forgotten. Maybe you've been gripping something that needs to be released to the Lord. It could be someone you love or something you feel you really need. Perhaps it is something you have been longing for, a long-sought dream you are hoping to achieve. Jehovah-Jireh, our provider, is ready to rattle your world—not to cruelly take away what you hold dear, but to lovingly place in your hands something so much greater.

CHAPTER 5

WHEN CALAMITY CRASHES IN

God's Wisdom When You Suffer Great Loss

THEY NEVER SAW IT COMING.

On a cold, quiet Saturday afternoon in a suburban township just outside Detroit, a family of four was getting ready to watch a movie together—mom, dad, and their son and daughter, ages two and four. Then, just before four o'clock, the upstairs playroom exploded in a ball of flames.

An airplane had crashed into their two-story home, tragically killing the pilot and two passengers. One moment that family was sitting cozily on their couch. The next moment they were fleeing for their lives. They went from comfort to calamity in a matter of seconds.[1]

Job never saw it coming either.

The catastrophe that crashed into his cozy, comfortable life jettisoned him into another world—the world of the impoverished, the stricken, the outcast. Though Job could never have anticipated the calamity upon calamity that tried to flatten him like a steamroller over asphalt, that didn't mean he wasn't prepared. In fact, Job had spent his life *staying* ready, so there was no need to *get* ready for whatever might come.

Most of us know Job's story. That stalwart man of faith and righteousness lost everything that mattered—his livelihood, his heirs, his social standing, and finally his health. He lost all the familiar landmarks of his life as he sat in brokenness and bankruptcy. To make matters worse, the God whom he had loved and worshiped all his life seemed not just silent but absent, and his few remaining friends heaped on judgment and bad advice—all based on bad theology.

In unguarded moments while sitting like a pile of discarded trash at the city dump, Job could easily have slipped into thoughts he had never entertained before: *Where is God? Why does He seem so distant? Does He even care? Does He even exist?*

Today, thousands of years after Job walked this earth, his story still resounds with relevance through the long corridors of history. As we visit the first two chapters of the book of Job to see how that man of God coped when calamity came crashing in, let me urge you to put yourself in his place. In the midst of disaster, instead of asking questions of God, let's ponder what God may be asking of us.

THE RIGHTEOUS MAN FROM UZ

The book of Job is easy to misread. People tend to speed through the first few verses as if they're just the opening credits of a movie before the real action kicks in. The shocking catastrophes are what leave their mark on our memories. In fact, if you do an Internet image search of "book of Job," the vast majority of results picture a morose, impoverished man, destitute and dejected—often with his "faithful" friends pointing fingers at him. That's how most of us picture him. A man sitting in a stinking mound of garbage, wearing ragged clothes, and with dirt on his head.

Yet without pondering the first two chapters—and especially the first five verses—we miss the whole point of this tragedy. In the opening lines we're introduced to the kind of man Job was prior to calamity crashing in. I know it's hard to paint a literal picture of a man with such a faultless character and flawless faith, but let's try to sketch a mental image of him *before* his calamities. Only then will the rest of the story make sense.

The book of Job begins, "There once was a man . . ." (1:1).

A *man*. Not a hero, not a superman, not a walking icon with a halo hovering over his head. Job is a mere mortal like you and me: frail, fallen, and with all the same weaknesses and temptations as anyone born of Adam's stock. Because Job is like us, nothing's stopping us from being like him.

Also notice that the author doesn't list any proud ancestry or famous family of origin. No "Job, son of _____." There's no indication that he's a member of an ancient aristocracy. He's not a prince or king. He's not even what we might call a "self-made man." His background isn't any more impressive than yours or mine.

He's just plain "Job."

Job hails from "the land of Uz" (Job 1:1). I find it interesting that nobody knows exactly where biblical Uz was located. Maybe somewhere in modern-day Jordan, maybe in Arabia, maybe beyond the Euphrates. Fascinating fact: when L. Frank Baum's book *The*

Wonderful Wizard of Oz was translated into Hebrew, they changed the name to *The Magician of Uz*.[2] No joke. It was probably a little pun by the translator—the land of Job might as well have been "somewhere over the rainbow"! But think about it. Job isn't from someplace special. You couldn't even find it on the map! Again, not much different from you and me.

Though that "average Job" comes from no lofty pedigree or impressive place, he is "blameless—a man of complete integrity" (Job 1:1). Not "sinless" or "perfect," but "blameless." That means if somebody tries to pin something on him, it won't stick. Or if somebody tries to trap him with a moral dilemma, he'll avoid the snare. He knows the right thing to do, and he does the right thing, regardless of the cost.

The mother of a friend of mine used to run the public utilities office in a small rural town. When my friend was a teenager, he used to pick her up after work. He'd often arrive a few minutes early and wait at the counter. His mother would watch the old office wall clock as the second hand slowly made its way to exactly four thirty. Then, on the dot, she'd gather her things, lock up the office, and leave for the day. When he asked why she didn't just leave a couple minutes early, she answered, "Some people in this town would love to have my job. And if they came at four twenty-nine and the office was closed, I'd just be giving them a basis to accuse me and get me fired."

That is how Job operates. He conducts himself in such a way that nobody can find a reason to accuse him. He does what is right in private and in public, even when nobody is around to see it.

How does he maintain his integrity and avoid evil? By fearing God (see Job 1:1). He stands out as a man of pure humility, moral fortitude, and ethical purity. If you do business with Job, you don't have to worry about "getting took." He can be trusted.

His God-fearing life is accompanied by a great reputation and many blessings. He has a large family of seven sons and three daughters (see Job 1:2), and he has become "the richest person in that entire area" (verse 3). There's no hint of hype or hyperbole in those words. So conscientious and other-focused is Job that he offers sacrifices to God on behalf of his ten adult children, saying, "Perhaps my children have sinned and have cursed God in their hearts" (verse 5).

He isn't so much "living the dream" as he is "reaping the harvest" of a life marked by authenticity, all the while holding those blessings loosely, with a heart of gratitude and selflessness. Though Job would never put himself up on a pedestal, I'm sure others in Uz could easily point to him as a "trophy" of God's workmanship displayed in his life of faith and obedience. The man is clear and clean to the core.

BEHIND THE CURTAINS

Imagine it's the opening night of a theatrical production. You're part of the audience. You flip though the playbill and orient yourself to the main characters and basic story line. The star of the show is a well-respected, highly skilled actor regarded by many as a genius of the craft. His past performances have been legendary.

As the lights dim, you expect the curtains to part and the performance to start. Instead, the director slips from between the curtains, draws the audience's attention, and fills you in on a plan the actors themselves know nothing about: the whole production is going to fall apart—*by design*.

It'll start with a few mechanical problems with the curtains and lights, followed by some misplaced props. Then certain characters will go missing. The actors will find themselves in unfamiliar sets and unexpected scenes. Eventually, characters will show up who have no part in the original script. The whole production, it turns out, is a test of the leading actor's ability to maintain composure, react on the fly, and hold to the maxim "The show must go on!"

It's the ultimate test of the main actor's talent.

In the same way, when the curtains open on that tragic day of Job's life in Job 1:13, he has no knowledge of the behind-the-scenes conversation that has taken place in verses 6 through 12. Those seven verses fill us readers in on some vital information that helps make sense of the rest of the story.

One day the members of the spiritual realm—angelic beings—assemble before God (see Job 1:6). Even the author of evil slithers in among them. The Hebrew calls him *ha satan*—literally, "the accuser"—from which we get the name "Satan." The book of Revelation looks forward to that day when heaven can rejoice with these glorious words: "The accuser of our brothers and sisters has been thrown down to earth—the one who accuses them before our God day and night" (12:10). Until then, Satan is apparently able to hound the saints in heaven's court like a nasty lawyer harassing people with a barrage of lawsuits.

The Lord calls Satan out: "Where have you come from?" (Job 1:7).

Satan, ever the sly devil, responds, "I have been patrolling the earth, watching everything that's going on" (1:7). Of course, we know this is a bit euphemistic. Satan wasn't just taking a leisurely stroll through the cities and towns of the world. The apostle Peter tells us that "the devil . . . prowls around like a roaring lion, looking for someone to devour" (1 Peter 5:8). His designs are always insidious.

At this point, God brings up Job as an example of integrity, purity, and humility. In fact, God says, "He is the finest man in all the earth. . . . He fears God and stays away from evil" (Job 1:8). What an endorsement!

But Satan counters that God's servant Job is in it only for the blessing, accusing God of putting a "wall of protection" around all his possessions. Who wouldn't walk with God when he's rolling in the dough? Who wouldn't find it easy to serve the Lord when he's being spoiled with wealth and security (1:9-10)? Satan casts doubt on Job's untested sincerity: "Reach out and take away everything he has, and he will surely curse you to your face" (verse 11).

I can just picture a sudden gasp rippling across that heavenly scene—or the angelic version of jaw-dropping. Satan has basically accused God of winning Job's worship by playing favorites—and accused Job of insincerity. Rip his comfort out from under him, Satan insists, and Job will crumple into a blasphemer in the blink of an eye!

For some reason, the Lord agrees to allow Satan to put that hypothesis to the test: "You may test him" (1:12). But he places limits on the scope of the testing. Satan has basically accused Job of being "in it for the money," so God allows Satan to take away all Job's earthly possessions, reducing him to poverty. But he is not permitted to harm him physically (see verse 12).

Satan exits the scene, on his way to strip Job of his wealth.

At that very moment, the curtains open, and we witness the effects of Satan's diabolical scheme.

THE FIRST ASSAULT

With hateful fury, Satan unleashes his initial shock-and-awe attack on Job with rapid-fire, back-to-back catastrophes.

That day, Job receives four messages in the course of just a few minutes—wave after wave of news that quickly goes from bad—to worse—to devastating—to life shattering! While one messenger is still speaking, the next rushes in.

First, Job learns that a raiding party of Sabeans has not only stolen his oxen and donkeys but killed all but one farmhand (see Job 1:14-15).

Next, he hears that some kind of fire has fallen from the sky and devoured both the sheep and the shepherds (1:16).

Then, Job is told that three bands of Chaldean raiders have stolen his camels and slaughtered his servants (1:17).

And finally—the worst news of all—a tornado has swept through and killed all of Job's children as they were feasting together in one house (1:18-19)!

How could anybody endure such a heartbreaking series of messages? Especially the last?

It reminds me of a scene in the World War II movie *Saving Private Ryan* when the mother of four sons sees a military vehicle kicking up dust as it winds its way to her farmhouse. An officer and a minister climb from the car as that trembling mother stands on the porch. A moment later, they deliver the news that not one, not two, but three of her four sons have fallen in battle within one week. Understandably, Mrs. Ryan collapses under the weight of the overwhelming anguish.

After ripping his robe in sorrow and shaving his head in mourning, Job, too, falls to the ground—but not in grief. He falls in worship (see Job 1:20)! This doesn't mean that he delights in his calamities or that he shrugs them off with a heartless ho hum. He is still mourning, like any of us would be. But he doesn't let his grief destroy his heavenly perspective. He doesn't let it demolish his theology.

Look at his astonishing response:

I came naked from my mother's womb,
    and I will be naked when I leave.
The LORD gave me what I had,
    and the LORD has taken it away.
Praise the name of the LORD!

JOB 1:21

Job never saw it coming.

He had no prior warning to get ready for the impending tragedy, no heads-up by an angel dispatched from the heavenly court. But he didn't need it, because he *stayed* ready for whatever calamity might come his way.

I wouldn't be surprised if it was Job's practice to thank God for all his blessings the moment he woke up each morning, to surrender them to the God who gave them, and to thank Him at the end of each day for all the people and possessions still on loan to him.

Like Job, we must always remember that God owns everything we have. When He chooses for whatever reason to remove some or all of it, He has every right to do so without an explanation. Consider the confession of King Nebuchadnezzar as he reflected on God taking away his sanity for a period of time:

> All the people of the earth
>   are nothing compared to him.
> He does as he pleases
>   among the angels of heaven
>   and among the people of the earth.
> No one can stop him or say to him,
>   "What do you mean by doing these things?"
>
> DANIEL 4:35

What a magnificent statement of God's majestic sovereignty!

Job recognizes that sovereignty too. He embraces it. Instead of stoking a sense of entitlement, he is more surprised than anybody at his prosperity.

Though Satan's flaming arrows have lit Job's life on fire, they have woefully missed their primary target: Job's faith. The chapter concludes, "In all of this, Job did not sin by blaming God" (Job 1:22).

After that onslaught of tragedies, I can hardly imagine how difficult it must have been for Job to explain it to his wife. I can picture him taking her in his arms, holding her close, and whispering, "Sweetheart, we've lost it all, including those precious ones we loved so much. But the One who loves us most of all has been so good to us. He has a reason for allowing this to happen. Maybe we'll never know why in this life, but we need to lean on Him through this."

A heartbroken Job and a grieving wife, along with a handful of shell-shocked servants, are the only ones left to bury their dead and reorder the chaos. Think about that. Grief-stricken, tears streaming down their faces, that elderly couple has to lay all their adult children to rest. One is bad enough, two would be horrible, three unimaginable. But all ten of them—gone.

THE SECOND ASSAULT

One thing's clear: Satan is a sore loser. He asked God to let him strip Job of his blessings with the expectation that Job would curse God. But instead, Job praises Him.

Rather than slinking away with his tail between his legs, Satan doubles down on his attacks. Never think he will back off forever. The adversary hates it when we continue in our walk with God, trusting Him through difficult times of pain and loss. We shouldn't be surprised when Satan unleashes wave after wave of calamities on God's people.

Even after his utter failure at tempting Jesus in the wilderness, Satan doesn't slither away in defeat. Luke tells us, "When the devil had finished tempting Jesus, he left him until the next opportunity came" (Luke 4:13). Let that sink in. If Satan will try to come at the God-man again after such an epic defeat, why would he stop with any of us after just one or two volleys?

We shouldn't be surprised that Satan returns to God's heavenly court for round two against Job.

The scene plays out almost exactly as it did the first time Satan accused Job. God uses the exact same description of Job he had used earlier—blameless and God fearing—but then adds, "He has maintained his integrity, even though you urged me to harm him without cause" (Job 2:3).

We know God isn't the one who harmed Job. But Satan could have done nothing to Job unless the Lord had removed His gracious hand of protection from him. When that happened, Satan rushed in with fury to strip Job of everything he held dear. Nothing good or bad happens to God's people outside His knowledge and without His permission.

In his response, Satan basically throws down the ultimate challenge: "Skin for skin! A man will give up everything he has to save his life. But reach out and take away his health, and he will surely curse you to your face!" (2:4-5). Satan basically asks God to remove every protection from Job to see if he really will maintain his faith.

God meets Satan's challenge. He gives permission: "All right, do with him as you please." Yet He has one condition: "Spare his life" (2:6).

Satan wastes no time. He takes off with plans to make Job even more miserable with a painful, debilitating skin disease: "He struck Job with terrible boils from head to foot" (2:7).

I've consulted commentaries on what, exactly, those "boils" were. Nobody really knows for sure. I even spoke with a dermatologist, and he said physicians have had a field day trying to diagnose that loathsome disease. Some say it could have been smallpox or elephantiasis. Maybe some form of acute eczema, leprosy, or psoriasis. Maybe pityriasis, keratosis, or pemphigus foliaceus. I don't even know what most of those are without googling them, but none of them sound good.

All we know for certain is that Job's malady is painful beyond belief. The text mentions a number of horrific symptoms. The boils cover his entire body (see Job 2:7). The persistent itching causes him to use a piece of broken pottery to scrape himself (2:8). The disease disfigures him to the point of being unrecognizable (2:12). The skin bursts open, scabs over, gets infected, and oozes with pus (7:5). Job loses his appetite (3:24), has difficulty breathing (9:18), and falls into fear and depression (3:24-26). I could go on, but you get the picture—horrible agony beyond telling.

Job has deteriorated so much that he ends up separated from the rest of society, living "among the ashes" (2:8). Warren Wiersbe gives some perspective on what that phrase means: "There the city garbage was deposited and burned, and there the city's rejects lived, begging alms from whoever passed by. At the ash heap, dogs fought over something to eat, and the city's dung was brought and burned. The city's leading citizen was now living in abject poverty and shame."[3]

UNWISE WORDS FROM JOB'S WIFE

From Job's limited perspective, this must be a season of complete confusion. He sits in isolation with no visible basis for hope and no way of changing his circumstances. Besides the external pain and internal turmoil Job faces, he also loses his wife's support. Her words churn with hopelessness: "Are you still trying to maintain your integrity? Curse God and die" (Job 2:9).

Before we castigate Mrs. Job, put yourself in her place for a moment. I know a lot of people who heroically endured personal pain and loss in their own lives but then faltered when they had to watch a close family member go through extreme suffering, even to the point of death. It's hard to see that, isn't it? Standing strong in the faith through your own debilitating disease is one thing; keeping your cool while a spouse or child is going through it is something else altogether.

Yes, Job's wife blurted out foolish words. But haven't we all had times when we wish we had bitten our tongues instead of spewing toxic words in a rash moment of irritation, pain, retaliation, or confusion? I'm sure you can remember such unrestrained outbursts.

We don't know for sure, but I believe Job's wife lived to regret those grief-drenched words. Don't forget that from her perspective, the end is near. She can't flip through to Job 42 and see how God will restore not only her husband's health but their family's fortune, blessing them with more children and grandchildren and great-grandchildren (see verses 10-17). As far as she knows, she could soon be a destitute widow rummaging through the filthy trash heaps herself.

So, she blurts out what she shouldn't have said. Unacceptable—but understandable. At that lowest point of her life, she is misery personified. Any one of us can plunge to that point given the right circumstances.

In light of the hasty words of Job's wife, let me pause to share two pieces of practical advice: one "always" and one "never." First, *always* guard your words when loved ones or friends are going through a grievous time. Think before you speak. You have no idea how your words might affect those who are hurting. You may think you're commiserating, sympathizing, putting words to their feelings, and standing beside them in their suffering. But what they actually need is somebody they can lean on, somebody who will simply sit in silence with them. If you feel you have to speak, they need words of strength and encouragement. What you say can affect them more than you realize, and even if you forget your comments later, your friends won't. Guard your words.

Second, *never* suggest that loved ones or friends compromise their integrity in hopes of finding relief. I've seen otherwise morally and theologically sound men and women so driven by desperation that they turn to illicit drugs to ease suffering. Or they run after superstitious treatments or theologically questionable remedies that go against everything they believe to be true. Never encourage that. They need wind beneath their wings, not weights around their necks.

JOB'S RESPONSE TO HIS CALAMITY

Back to Job. His response after all the loss and pain reverberates through the ages.

First, he has a reproof for his wife: "You talk like a foolish woman" (Job 2:10). She tries to push him over the edge; Job pushes back. Notice that even in his rebuke, Job is gentle. He doesn't tell her to shut up, doesn't send her away, and doesn't directly say, "You're a fool." He says her *words* are like those spoken by a fool. She needs his tender correction, and Job treats her with grace and mercy even in his reproof.

Second, look at Job's reaction and resolve: "Should we accept only good things from the hand of God and never anything bad?" (2:10). I wish every health-and-wealth preacher would remember that line—print it, frame it, and hang it in their opulent offices. It reflects a sound theology of the sovereignty of God, His wisdom, and His power. It also reflects a man who's so firm in faith that even in his horrifying condition, he can keep a strong grip on his theology, knowing God is keeping a strong grip on him.

Psalm 115:3 says, "Our God is in the heavens, and he does as he wishes." This is Job's theology, and he doesn't forget it even from the trash heap. He is able to accept whatever will glorify God, regardless of how he feels about it. He knows God doesn't work in our lives only to make us happy. He works in our lives to grow us into people like His Son, who "learned obedience from the things he suffered" (Hebrews 5:8).

I love the author's endorsement of Job's response: "In all this, Job said nothing wrong" (Job 2:10). It's the equivalent of those glorious words you and I hope to hear one day from our Lord and Savior: "Well done, my good and faithful servant" (Matthew 25:21).

Job's theology holds fast.

His determination remains strong.

No wonder the Lord called him "the finest man in all the earth" (Job 1:8).

WHAT TO DO WHEN CALAMITY CRASHES IN

In light of the example of Job, I'd like to share three truths that will help us walk in the path he cut for us through his own crushing calamities. With these principles firmly in mind, you'll be better prepared when similar tragedies invade your own life. They are foundational theological truths, but they're also powerfully practical. No doubt, you've heard them before—and you'll hear them again. But these foundation stones have a tendency to come loose when the floodwater of adversity comes crashing in over and over again. It's vital to keep them firm and fixed in your heart and mind. I'll state each theological truth, then follow it with a "so what" application.

1. **Our trials are inevitable.** So, *don't be surprised* when they come. You may have suffered trials far worse than I've ever suffered. My heart goes out to you. I salute you for your

endurance, but more trials are coming. A minister named Robert Alden put it this way: "This is a hard lesson for some believers to learn, especially if they feel they have been promised health and wealth or have (mis)understood that God's wonderful plan for their lives involves only pleasantness and not trouble."[4] Job knew better, and so should we. Our trials are inevitable.

2. **Our friends are fallible.** So, *don't be fooled* when well-meaning loved ones give you bad advice. They have just as limited a perspective as you do. And they're just as susceptible to error as anyone else. Our world is fallen. We're all imperfect. Job got bad advice from his wife. We give bad advice to others. And others will certainly give bad advice to us. Don't rest your confidence on those words. Rest on His Word.

3. **Our God is sovereign.** So, *don't be disillusioned* when life hits hard. During the seasons of peace and blessing, prepare yourself spiritually for whatever may come. It's too late for a soldier to learn how to fire his weapon in the midst of the raging battle. And it's too late for believers to firm up their view of the sovereignty of God in the midst of life's fiery trials. When your life is free of trouble, don't become complacent. When calamity crashes in, don't be disillusioned. He's preparing you to stand before Him, looking more like His Son than you did at the start.

When calamity crashes in, remember Job. With his feet firmly fixed on solid theology, he stayed ready for whatever winds of calamity blew in. Follow his example. Place your feet on these stead-fast theological foundation stones, and lean into the trials with hope:

- Our trials are inevitable; don't be surprised.
- Our friends are fallible; don't be fooled.
- Our God is sovereign; don't be disillusioned.

Having that good theology in place helped Job *stay* ready so that when calamity came, he didn't have to *get* ready. And it can do the same for you.

CHAPTER 6

WHEN GOD GIVES GRACE TO ENDURE

God's Wisdom When You Are Touched by Trauma

THEY BEGIN WITH A SEEMINGLY IMPOSSIBLE EXPERIENCE—one so bleak you could never have predicted it—let alone plan for it. In our day, they're the stuff of niche insurance policies or prime-time docudramas. Jaw-dropping, head-shaking, shiver-in-your-boots kinds of trauma that drive even atheists to pray.

Though floods or fires can leave us homeless, we can rebuild. And while fraud or theft can leave us penniless, we can recover financially. But horrific experiences like sexual assault; parental abandonment; and mental, emotional, or physical abuse leave us deeply scarred. They take more than our property; they strip us of our confidence, dignity, and security. In some cases, they rob us even of our faith and hope.

Most people have experienced some kind of trauma in their lives.

Perhaps you have suffered abuse at the hands of bullies, strangers, or those who were supposed to love and protect you. Some people earn the title "survivor" due to the depth of wickedness they have endured. In the midst of those cruel seasons of suffering and their aftermath, it's certainly easy to wonder, *Where was God?*

Yet even in the darkest places, the light of God's grace blazes like a pillar of fire in the night. He intervenes and brings beauty from ugliness, purpose from pain, and comfort from sorrow. In these difficult times, accounts of God's faithfulness can minister to our spirits. They narrate a vital truth about God's grace for enduring even the most anguishing hardships and crushing cruelties.

The story of Joseph is one such encouraging account. Here, we see a man of God repeatedly beaten up and broken down. As a young adult he's battered and bartered by his own brothers—an experience that would have emotionally scarred the best of us. Yet instead of seething with rage and seeking revenge, Joseph shifts his focus to the living God, who gives grace to endure.

Joseph's experiences of abuse and abandonment speak to us today—as do his responses, which flowed from a firm belief in the sovereignty and goodness of God. If you have "been there," you can learn to discern God's grace to endure even the toughest trials. And when you're ministering to others reeling from injury and injustice, you'll have insight into how to point them to the source of Joseph's strength.

A HISTORY OF CALAMITIES

Joseph's tribulations begin with abuse and abandonment at age seventeen (see Genesis 37:2). Think about that. *Just seventeen!* As we recount Joseph's story, think about how you, at seventeen, would have responded to the mistreatment he faced.

Because of jealousy, Joseph's older siblings long to rid themselves of their annoying brother once and for all. In a rash moment, they decide to murder him (see verses 18-20). Not tease him. Not harass him. Not even beat him up to teach him a lesson. *Murder!* It sounds like a post from our own twenty-first-century news feeds! Human nature hasn't really changed, has it?

Thankfully, unchecked envy hasn't seared the conscience of every member of that rogue band of brothers. Reuben steps up on behalf of his younger brother and convinces the rest to dump Joseph into a cistern and leave him for dead (see verses 21-24).

Suddenly they see a camel caravan in the distance—Ishmaelite traders on their way to Egypt (see verse 25). The conspiracy to commit murder suddenly shifts to an ancient case of human trafficking. Why let Joseph rot in a pit like a bag of garbage when there is money to be had? In a great plot twist, Joseph ends up loaded onto one of the traders' camels (see verses 26-28). We can only imagine the abusive treatment Joseph might have endured at the hands of the Ishmaelites during that long trek to Egypt.

IN THE DEPTHS—MINUS DESPAIR

From favored son to forgotten slave, Joseph's descent into darkness is just getting started. In a matter of days, that privileged teenager goes from the familiar land of promise to a strange country with a language he doesn't understand, customs he can't comprehend, and bizarre gods he can't fathom. He finds himself sold to a man named Potiphar, Pharaoh's captain of the guard (see Genesis 37:36).

How easy it would be for Joseph to feed the flames of bitterness and vengeance, to plot his retaliation against everybody who has wronged him—from his hateful brothers to the caravan of low-life traders. How natural it would be for him to sit in darkness and replay the abuse and abandonment over and over in his mind, seething in deeper rage with each pass through those unjust injuries. It would be understandable if Joseph were to lie night after night on a cold, hard rug, thinking, *You just wait. My day is coming. You haven't seen the last of me!*

Perhaps you have no trouble imagining such a natural response to abuse and injustice. Maybe reflecting on Joseph's experience as a teen feels like pouring salt on the open wounds of your own past injuries. Maybe you've known such cruelty, been the victim of life-shattering abuse. In unguarded moments, your pain pulsates and penetrates your thoughts, overwhelms your emotions, and takes charge of your mind. You find yourself thinking, saying, and feeling things nobody should have to think, say, or feel.

We can sympathize with Joseph. We would understand if he took pleasure in mulling over his abuse in those long midnight hours, alone in his thoughts. Plotting his escape. Planning his payback.

But he doesn't.

Not once.

In the depths of his undeserved suffering, Joseph shows no signs of harbored hatred.

Think about that. Even as life deals him additional blows and setbacks, he keeps his cool. He is seventeen or eighteen years old now. No father to love him and lend mature advice. No mother to comfort him. No family to protect him.

Then, when a powerful seductress tries to take advantage of him, he repeatedly resists (see Genesis 39:6-10). In return, she falsely accuses him of attempted rape and has him cast into prison (see verses 11-20).

In that dungeon, Joseph lends spiritual guidance to Pharaoh's imprisoned cupbearer, leading to the man's release and reinstatement. Instead of using his position of influence to rescue Joseph from jail, that "friend" reneges on his promise and forgets all about Joseph (see Genesis 40:1-23).

What a litany of abuses and injustices Joseph endured!

- attacked by his brothers
- sold into slavery
- sexually harassed
- falsely accused of rape
- wrongfully imprisoned
- betrayed by a friend

Talk about being put through the wringer!

How in the world could anybody—let alone a man in his late teens and early twenties—endure such treatment without shaking his fist at God or lifting his hand against his enemies?

HEROIC ENDURANCE

When we follow the often-harrowing exploits of the men and women of faith throughout the Bible, it's easy to picture them as heroes. Maybe something in their DNA set them apart from the rest of us— still mortal, yes, but mortal plus *something supernatural*.

Or maybe their moral fabric was woven from a stronger thread than those of us who barely make it through a day without staining our mediocre character with sin.

Or perhaps their life experiences instilled in them a tried-and-true fortitude the rest of us lack in our average upbringing.

Not so!

Only as recipients of God's merciful salvation and gracious empowerment were the saints of old able to endure their intense hardships. If we were to write God's role out of the saga of human history, the drama wouldn't make it out of Genesis 3. From Adam, to Noah, to Abraham, to Jacob, to Joseph, to Moses, to David and the promised Messiah—God was at work. Sometimes in obvious, supernatural ways, but often behind the scenes.

The real hero of the Bible, then, is the living God.

Yet as we peer into the life of Joseph in the latter chapters of Genesis, it would be easy to think that God has abandoned him somewhere between the pit and the prison. It would certainly be natural for Joseph himself to reach that conclusion.

But *natural* has nothing to do with Joseph's situation and his responses. God's *supernatural* presence—though cloaked in the cause and effect of everyday life—can be spotted throughout these pages by those who have eyes to see and ears to hear.

FIVE FATEFUL WORDS

In the tale of Joseph, God doesn't abscond from His providential presence nor abdicate His sovereign rule. He is there, all the way through. Over and over and over again, He makes His presence known both in the details of the scenes and in the overarching narrative.

In our review of Joseph's life-altering trauma, we skipped over five vital words interjected at key moments of the narrative: *The Lord was with Joseph.*

The promise of God's presence brings the needed comfort and encouragement to endure. The first time I grasped the magnitude of this promise was in the Marine Corps. I was on a troop ship crossing the Pacific Ocean, bound for southeast Asia, and the journey took seventeen days. The ocean swells on stormy days were sometimes fifty feet high. When our ship was down at the base of the swell, the crest loomed above like a giant mountain about to collapse on us. As we rose up to the peak again, we could see nothing but water all around—deep, blue-black swells as far as the eye could see in every direction. It left me feeling alone and uneasy.

I remember opening my Bible early one morning to the Psalms:

I can never escape from your Spirit!
    I can never get away from your presence!
If I go up to heaven, you are there;
    if I go down to the grave, you are there.
If I ride the wings of the morning,
    if I dwell by the farthest oceans,
even there your hand will guide me,
    and your strength will support me.

PSALM 139:7-10

When I saw those words, I almost shouted for joy. The promise of His presence and protection comforted me like nothing else. All thoughts of loneliness and fear fled away. His hand was leading me, holding tightly to me right there in the "farthest oceans." Even though the surrounding swells could have swallowed me up in a moment, the five-word promise that "the Lord was with me" swept over me with a calming assurance.

Those same five words of promise strengthened Joseph as well.

Does this mean a blaze of fire followed Joseph everywhere he went? Did he hear a voice assuring him of God's protection and provision? Did he have an inexplicable warmth in his chest, reminding him of the Lord's abiding love?

No. Look at the evidence of God's steadfast presence in Joseph's life: "*The LORD was with Joseph*, so he succeeded in everything he did as he served in the home of his Egyptian master. Potiphar noticed this and realized that *the LORD was with Joseph*, giving him success in everything he did" (Genesis 39:2-3, emphasis added). The effects of God's presence with Joseph are seen in the blessing he experienced as he managed Potiphar's household (see verse 5).

Before we regard all success and prosperity as clear signs of God's presence, we need to recall that in one day Joseph lost it all—under the cruel false accusations of Potiphar's wife (39:19-20)! Yet even then, we see continued signs of God's loving, merciful, gracious presence: "But *the LORD was with Joseph* in the prison and showed him his faithful love. And the LORD made Joseph a favorite with the prison warden" (verse 21, emphasis added). The warden put Joseph in charge of the other prisoners, promoting him to a position of leadership, and "*the LORD was with him* and caused everything he did to succeed" (verse 23).

God's abiding presence didn't translate into a sudden rescue from slavery or release from prison. Instead, *even in the depths, God's grace provided the power to endure.* In fact, where the natural man—a man who did not trust in God—would have despaired and perished, God caused Joseph to depend on Him and flourish.

The seeds of blessing planted in the soil of Joseph's suffering finally came to fruition thirteen years after he was sold into slavery. Let that sink in. *For thirteen years*—from the age of seventeen to the age of thirty (see Genesis 37:2; 41:46)—Joseph's situation wavered between tortuous and tolerable.

Joseph waited.

And waited.

And waited some more.

All the while, *the Lord was with Joseph.* This truth gave Joseph the grace to endure with faith and hope, like a ripening fruit abiding in a nourishing vine.

HOPE OF RELIEF

The Lord gave Joseph grace to endure both the bombardment of tragedies and the year-after-year languishing in prison. Yet He wasn't finished with him. Not by a long shot. God had greater plans for him than merely managing an Egyptian jailhouse.

At one point in his tenure as warden's assistant, Joseph exhibited his relationship with the living God by interpreting the dreams of Pharaoh's imprisoned chief baker and chief cupbearer (see Genesis 40). When he relayed the favorable interpretation of the cupbearer's dream, which led to the man's release from prison, Joseph requested, "Please remember me and do me a favor when things go well for you. Mention me to Pharaoh, so he might let me out of this place" (verse 14).

Joseph's words show no spite, no complaining, and no panicked pleading for rescue. At the same time, though, he knows freedom is better than imprisonment, justice better than injustice, and vindication better than underserved punishment. Yes, by God's sustaining grace, Joseph has come to terms with his condition and made the most of it. But this doesn't extinguish his righteous longing for relief and release.

When we choose to share Joseph's perspective, we can have the same attitude toward our own adverse situations. We're not called to wallow in our sufferings like those who lose confidence in God's goodness—or lose hope in His plan. Neither are we called to relish our pain, call our bad situation good, or plug our ears, close our eyes, and mindlessly shout "lalalalala!" to avoid what we don't want to acknowledge. Joseph displayed endurance. But like anybody shuffling through the tangled weeds of suffering, he longed for a clear path of relief. There's nothing wrong with that. When God sends a way out, take it!

JOSEPH'S NEW ROBE—AND ROLE

Sure enough, the chief cupbearer "forgot all about Joseph, never giving him another thought" (40:23). As we would expect, Joseph lets another opportunity for bitterness and resentment slip by. Despite the abuse, false accusation, and betrayal, Joseph continues to trust in God, to live the life He has for him, and to leave his burdens at His feet. Instead of seething with anger toward the cupbearer, Joseph rests on the grace of God to endure the unfairness of his situation.

Then we read a great word of relief in the account of Joseph's calamities: *finally*.

Two years after the cupbearer forgot all about his promise to Joseph, Pharaoh has disturbing dreams that leave his own magicians and wise men dumbfounded (see Genesis 41:1-8). In the midst of their "above our pay grade" silence, the king's chief cupbearer "*finally* . . . spoke up" (verse 9).

Finally! The cupbearer tells Pharaoh about that forsaken "young Hebrew man" in jail who can interpret dreams (41:9-13). Immediately, Joseph is whisked from prison and brought before the ruler (see verses 14-15). When Pharaoh asks Joseph to interpret his dreams, Joseph replies with humility: "It is beyond my power to do this. . . . But God can tell you what it means and set you at ease" (verse 16).

After hearing Pharaoh's mysterious dreams (see Genesis 41:17-24), Joseph informs him that after seven years of abundance, seven years of famine will hit Egypt (verses 25-32). Along with this revelation, Joseph offers some advice: put somebody wise in charge of gathering and storing excess grain to be used during the time of famine (see verses 33-36).

Marveling at Joseph's Spirit-endowed wisdom, Pharaoh exclaims, "Since God has revealed the meaning of the dreams to you, clearly no one else is as intelligent or wise as you are. You will be in charge of my court, and all my people will take orders from you. Only I, sitting on my throne, will have a rank higher than yours" (41:39-40).

What a twist! Just an hour earlier, Joseph was imprisoned in a dungeon. Now he is promoted to a place higher than any official in the kingdom except Pharaoh himself! Joseph is decked out in fine royal linen, given Pharaoh's signet ring as a sign of authority, and provided with a chariot for travel throughout Egypt. Nothing happens in Egypt now without his approval (41:42-44).

From prisoner to prince, Joseph's long-awaited redemption has *finally* come. And what is Joseph thinking as he leads Egypt in preparing for the famine? We get a rare glimpse of his mature mind through the names of the two sons born to him and his Egyptian wife. The first he named Manasseh, which means "causing to forget," because "God has made me forget all my troubles and everyone in my father's family" (41:51). The second child he named Ephraim, which means "fruitful," because "God has made me fruitful in this land of my grief" (verse 52).

FULL CIRCLE

With Joseph exalted to the second-highest position in the land of Egypt, the biblical scene cuts back to his family in Canaan, reeling under the devastating effects of the famine (see Genesis 42:1). After learning that Egypt has a stockpile of grain for sale, Jacob sends Joseph's ten older brothers—minus his youngest brother, Benjamin—to purchase some to keep them alive (see verses 1-5).

When they arrive, Joseph recognizes them (see Genesis 42:7), but none of his siblings has any inkling that it is their younger brother—sold into slavery over twenty years earlier—who is standing over them at that moment. In a dramatic series of tests likely intended to determine what kind of men his brothers had become over the past two decades, Joseph accuses them of espionage while also blessing them with the provisions they need (see Genesis 42:8–44:34).

While Joseph is putting his brothers to the test with temporary imprisonment, demands that they fetch their younger brother, and false accusations of treachery, he catches a glimpse of their shame for how they had treated him all those years ago.

Speaking among themselves, they said, "Clearly we are being punished because of what we did to Joseph long ago. We saw his anguish when he pleaded for his life, but we wouldn't listen. That's why we're in this trouble."

"Didn't I tell you not to sin against the boy?" Reuben asked. "But you wouldn't listen. And now we have to answer for his blood!"

GENESIS 42:21-22

Because they are conversing in their own Hebrew language, they assume Joseph won't understand them (see Genesis 42:23). Even though Joseph is moved to tears at their admission of guilt, he continues the ruse in order to get them to bring their youngest brother, Benjamin, to Egypt, keeping Simeon as collateral. Still, not a single brother recognizes Joseph.

Fast-forward to the climax of this great drama. Joseph has orchestrated a roller-coaster ride of emotions, but the time has come for the "great reveal." So, while they are standing before him with their hats in their hands, begging for mercy, Joseph dismisses his attendants, breaks down in tears, and exclaims, "I am Joseph! . . . Is my father still alive?" (45:3).

JOSEPH'S VERTICAL PERSPECTIVE

In that moment, the brothers' guilt changes to terror. Their first reaction is understandable. They are stunned speechless (45:3). I'm sure several of them think they are facing not a merciful brother but a merciless executioner. From a purely natural point of view, they have every reason to think so. Why wouldn't Joseph want revenge?

Why wouldn't he take this opportunity to wield his power and put them down? This is payback time! Why not do to them what they had done to him?

Joseph calls them closer and says, "Don't be upset, and don't be angry with yourselves for selling me to this place. It was God who sent me here ahead of you to preserve your lives. . . . God has sent me ahead of you to keep you and your families alive and to preserve many survivors. So it was God who sent me here, not you!" (45:5, 7-8).

Joseph could justly avenge himself for their wickedness. Instead, he schools them in sound theology. While he has every right to be angry, he urges them, "Don't be angry with yourselves" (45:5). Over and over he tells them, "God sent me . . . God sent me . . . God sent me." I can imagine those thirteen years of calamity flashing before Joseph's tear-filled eyes. Yet each event—and all of them together—has been ordained and orchestrated by God to bring Joseph and his brothers to *this* point.

Even after Joseph has used his influence to resettle his entire family, including his father, Jacob, in Egypt, his brothers wonder when the other shoe will drop. Though Joseph's words and actions demonstrate forgiveness and grace, it is difficult for them to accept his love. When Jacob dies years later, they brace themselves for the worst: "But now that their father was dead, Joseph's brothers became fearful. 'Now Joseph will show his anger and pay us back for all the wrong we did to him,' they said" (50:15). They are certain Joseph has been biding time until his father is gone; now he will mete out just punishment to his abusers. They beg for forgiveness, plead for mercy, and offer themselves to Joseph as slaves (see verses 16-18). They are convinced he will soon finish them off.

Instead, Joseph reaffirms his theology with these remarkable, reassuring words: "Am I God, that I can punish you? You intended to harm me, but God intended it all for good. He brought me to this position so I could save the lives of many people. No, don't be afraid. I will continue to take care of you and your children" (50:19-21).

This is one of the clearest examples in all the Bible of a *vertical* instead of a *horizontal* perspective. I'm sure this point of view isn't a sudden epiphany to Joseph. No, he has believed in the long-range view throughout his life, even when he had no clear evidence to support it. His firm theology of God's goodness, wisdom, and sovereignty leads him to believe that despite the terrible calamities he has endured, God has a purpose behind them. This is why he makes it through those thirteen years of tribulation with no trace of self-pity, anger, vengeance, bitterness, or resentment.

GRACE IN ACTION

I'll confess, as I reflect on this whole account, I have an easier time thinking like Joseph's brothers than like Joseph. Maybe you do too.

If given the chance to get even with those who have harmed us in ways that altered the course and quality of our lives, I wonder if you and I could say like Joseph, "God's in control. He knows best. I choose forgiveness." In the abstract, we'd like to think we would say, "Of course I choose forgiveness." But in reality, we are often more likely to come up with reasons why this particular person or that particular trauma warrants an exception to Joseph-level grace and mercy.

Like his brothers, we're also great at reminding ourselves of the wrongs we've done in our own lives. Maybe you can't let yourself forget your failures. Or maybe there's someone you've mistreated or assailed with ugly words. Or maybe you've treated someone unjustly. Too often, we're like Joseph's brothers, begging over and over and over again for God's mercy. Fearful that we're just one misstep away from His wrath. Worried that He will strike us down.

If you're feeling buried under your own sin, there's no way you can dig yourself out of the hole. Don't even try. On your own, you're done for. But along comes our gracious, loving God, who sent His Son to secure forgiveness and peace about our shortcomings and failures. When Jesus went to that cross, died, and paid your penalty, He took care of it all—past, present, and future.

How quickly we forget God's grace!

I love what Frederick Buechner writes about grace:

Grace is something you can never get but can only be given. There's no way to earn it or deserve it or bring it about any more than you can deserve the taste of raspberries and cream or earn good looks or bring about your own birth. . . .

A crucial eccentricity of the Christian faith is the assertion that people are saved by grace. There's nothing *you* have to do. There's nothing you *have* to do. There's nothing you have to *do*.[1]

Grace can't be earned. God doesn't owe us His blessings, and we couldn't pay Him back for them even if He expected us to. The proper response to God's grace is gratitude.

Joseph understood what his brothers didn't. He had been a recipient of God's grace to endure. He had been brought low, then highly exalted. He knew the right response was to pay it forward. His brothers were operating on the philosophy "you get what you deserve." So, Joseph offered them the same grace God had given him.

What a stunning portrait of grace in action. Joseph didn't just wish for it or imagine it or think, "Someday I'm going to put grace into action and let my brothers know that I forgive them." No, he actually forgave them. He refused to lick his wounds and bear a grudge. He looked those brothers in the eye and refused to play God with their lives. Joseph truly demonstrated the grace to forgive and press on.

THREE PILLARS OF ENDURANCE

Though they're not explicit in Scripture, I see three pillars of Joseph's theology that led to his ability to endure every hardship without bitterness. These pillars aren't spelled out clearly for us. We have to read between the lines. But they're fundamental truths about God that help us make sense of Joseph's words and actions. As we grow to embrace these truths, they'll provide the same kind of stability in our lives as they did in Joseph's.

1. **Joseph saw God's perfect plan in every location.** He said, "It was God who sent me here ahead of you to preserve your lives" (Genesis 45:5). It wouldn't have taken Joseph long to think through the places he had to go in order to end up where he was. Had he not been in that caravan of Ishmaelites, he wouldn't have ended up in Egypt. If he

hadn't ended up in Egypt, he wouldn't have wound up in Potiphar's house. If he hadn't been in Potiphar's house, he wouldn't have landed in prison. If he hadn't been in prison, he wouldn't have been summoned to Pharaoh's palace. If he hadn't been called to Pharoah's palace, he wouldn't have been appointed as second in command. Joseph could look back and see God's perfect plan in every location. Each link in the chain connecting one place to another depended on the one before.

2. **Joseph sensed God's gracious hand in every position.** He said, "God has made me master over all the land of Egypt" (Genesis 45:9). Regardless of how far down circumstances tried to drag Joseph, God saw to it that he would eventually rise above them. When Joseph was sold as a slave to Potiphar, the Lord was with him, giving him success and favor. His master promoted Joseph to a position of "personal attendant . . . in charge of his entire household and everything he owned" (39:4). Then, when Joseph was cast into prison, the blessing of God upon him propelled him to a position where he was "in charge of all the other prisoners and over everything that happened in the prison" (39:22). Not only was Joseph in the right place at the right time, but he was in the right position at each critical juncture in the unfolding of God's plan.

3. **Joseph submitted to God's sovereign will in every situation.** He said, "God intended it all for good" (Genesis 50:20). Talk about an attitude that makes all the difference in the world! Joseph acknowledged that God was in it all, from

start to finish. From the dark cistern in Canaan—to the dungeon cell in Egypt—to the right hand of Pharaoh's throne. Because of this perspective, Joseph refused to punish his brothers for their wickedness (see verse 19). This didn't mean that what they did was good. They intended it for evil (50:20). Yet even their intentionally wicked acts were redeemed by God and woven into the tapestry of His plan.

I can remember a time early on in my seminary training when the doctrine of the sovereignty of God frightened me. Didn't it mean that God is a distant deity? Or a celestial brute, pushing and maneuvering His way through nameless humanity?

Through a series of events far too numerous and complicated to describe, I've come to realize that, rather than being frightened by God's sovereignty, I'm now comforted in it. Since He alone is God, and since He, being God, has good as His goal, how could I do anything but embrace it?

God gives us grace to endure. And it is *providential, sovereign* grace. In all the mystery of His waiting and working, He can still be trusted. Like Joseph did in Egypt, you and I must remain sensitive to those moments when He will finally break the silence and intervene on our behalf. And while we're waiting in hope to reach our destination, we must endure the journey, day after day, in faith.

CHAPTER 7

WHEN THE GIANTS
OF LIFE ATTACK

God's Wisdom When You Face Insurmountable Challenges

PEOPLE LIKE TO PULL FOR UNDERDOGS. You know who I mean.

Think of the American Revolution, when a ragtag army of colonists stood against the well-equipped redcoats and won their independence from England.

Or recall the "Miracle on Ice" at the 1980 Winter Olympics, when an unknown group of American hockey players whipped the "undefeatable" Soviets at their own game.

These and countless other stories of unexpected heroes rising to the occasion line the shelves of bookstores and draw crowds at movie theaters. The underdogs, with the odds stacked against them, somehow pull off an astonishing victory. This moving theme undergirds the plots of historic blockbusters like *Star Wars*, *Rocky*, and *The Karate Kid*.

Yes, we love underdog stories.

That is, as long as we're not the underdogs.

The mentality tends to shift when we're the ones outnumbered, outweighed, or outmaneuvered. More often than not, instead of standing tall, we slink away. Instead of drumming up optimism, we slip into cynicism. Instead of charging the hill, we retreat into an attitude of defeat. Left all alone, we begin to feel reluctant, overwhelmed, intimidated. We prepare for loss before we've even entered the fray.

Strange how that works, isn't it? We love the stories of *other* underdogs taking on the Big Dog, but all too often we believe those stunning victories could never happen to us.

God preserved an account in Scripture that sheds light on this classic underdog dilemma. Though true, the story has become a metaphor for any against-all-odds confrontation between a little guy and a giant.[1] How often have we heard people refer to a situation as a "David and Goliath" moment? And how deeply they long for "David" to win!

Yet if observers standing on that ancient field of battle had been taking bets on the outcome, nobody would have placed a wager on David.

REAL GIANTS

I'll never forget the day I met a real giant.

Years ago, Cynthia and I vacationed with several family members on the small island of Kauai, Hawaii. I got up one morning for an early jog along the beach, opened the door of our hotel room, and stepped into the hallway. To my absolute shock, standing before me was a seven-foot-two real-life giant!

The true shock was, I had just watched that giant win the NBA championship with the LA Lakers a couple weeks earlier. There he stood, staring down at me—basketball legend Kareem Abdul-Jabbar.

That man not only had a giant reputation, but his looming presence made me feel like I had just shrunk several inches.

When my heart started beating again, I realized he wasn't at all the mythical giant I had made him out to be. You see, he had misplaced the key to his room, just like every average Joe does a dozen times while vacationing. There he was, roaming the hallway to see if he or his wife had dropped it somewhere along the way.

Believe it or not, it turned out that his key was on the floor in *our* room, just inside the entrance. His wife had slid it under the door, thinking our room was theirs.

So much for giants. After a few friendly words, we went our separate ways. I still chuckle a bit when I remember that encounter.

Now, wouldn't it be great if we could just laugh off all of life's giants?

While we can avoid some imposing confrontations, we can't dodge them all. And often, running isn't an option. This is especially true when giants threaten us and our families. With so much at stake, we have to take a stand.

Let's return together to one of the most familiar stories in the Bible—so well known that people who have never cracked open Holy Scripture have heard about it. Though this story deals with a real giant named Goliath and a real underdog named David, it illustrates a vital lesson about facing the inevitable giants of our own lives.

That lesson is summed up in 1 John 4:4—"You belong to God, my dear children. You have already won a victory over those people, because the Spirit who lives in you is greater than the spirit who lives in the world."

We all deal with giants from time to time. And even though none of them are nine feet tall, clad in armor, and roaming the streets in our neighborhood, that doesn't make them any less real. Most of the time they're not even people, but terrifying situations, exasperating circumstances, frightening challenges, or threatening experiences. Though they have no proper names, they're giants, nonetheless.

Are you ready to face the intimidating giants in your life? Have you had enough of cowering and caving to their invasive intimidation?

If so, read on.

A (TOO-)FAMILIAR TALE

The story of David and Goliath in 1 Samuel 17 is fifty-eight verses packed with tension, drama, suspense, action, twists, and even a touch of humor. No wonder people young and old have been drawn to it over the centuries.

The story is familiar to us. Maybe too familiar. Sometimes we miss important details in its over-telling. Like me, you may have heard the story for the first time in Sunday school class, read it in children's Bible storybooks, or seen it in a cartoon. However, we rarely explore the nooks and crannies of the biblical account. When we do, we notice interesting and important details that might cast the story in a different light.

Let's start with the chapter right before Goliath shows up. An important principle in 1 Samuel 16 puts the whole encounter in perspective.

As the prophet Samuel zeroes in on the Lord's choice to replace King Saul, God leads him to the household of Jesse in Bethlehem. After taking one look at Jesse's son Eliab, Samuel thinks, "Surely this is the LORD's anointed!" (1 Samuel 16:6). Apparently, Eliab was quite a sight—tall, strong, and handsome.

God quickly turns Samuel's attention away from Eliab with these great words: "Don't judge by his appearance or height, for I have rejected him. The LORD doesn't see things the way you see them. People judge by outward appearance, but the LORD looks at the heart" (16:7).

Never forget that! This principle holds true for all people at all times. We're often impressed with appearances, intimidated by strength, and overwhelmed by a person's fame, fortune, or title. We forget that none of those features matter to God. He doesn't judge people by what's on the outside but by the authenticity of their lives and the condition of their hearts.

That's why God chooses David from among Jesse's sons. That kid is so far off Jesse's radar as a candidate for kingship that he doesn't even bother to parade him past the prophet with the rest of his sons (see 1 Samuel 16:8-11). When God rejects every one of Jesse's boys, Samuel asks if they are all he has. Jesse replies, "There is still the youngest. . . . But he's out in the fields watching the sheep and goats" (verse 11).

Classic underdog.

As soon as David arrives, God speaks: "This is the one; anoint him" (16:12).

I can imagine David's older brothers turning a little green with envy as that ceremonial oil runs down David's neck and back, marking him as the future king of Israel. Even his own father wouldn't have guessed it. Probably David himself has only the faintest idea what is going on.

But God has a plan for that underdog, and His opinion is all that matters.

A STUDY IN CONTRASTS

We often hear of the obvious contrasts between King Saul and David—the one tall, strong, dashing, and brought up in a rich, influential family—the other young, unknown, probably of average build, a music lover, who grew up tending his father's flocks. Saul fits the bill as a king like those of the nations around Israel—someone who *looks and acts* like a leader (see 1 Samuel 8:20). We can understand why the masses would want a king like Saul—and why David's own father overlooks that lanky shepherd lad.

We can understand it—until we see those superficial differences proved in the fires of a real test of character.

A bit of time has passed since David's anointing. He is back in the fields, watching over his father's sheep and goats. Saul is still king, flip-flopping his way through politics and power, wrestling his own demons, which threaten to undo him.

Meanwhile, the valley of Elah has erupted into conflict. The Philistines assemble on one side of that ravine; the army of Israel encamps on the other.

Enter the massive giant of Gath: Goliath. That champion of the Philistine army stands just a few inches shy of a basketball rim—over nine and a half feet tall. His thick coat of mail weighs 125 pounds; the head of his spear alone weighs 15.

In the reaction to Goliath we find the real study in contrasts—the canyon-wide difference between Saul's floundering and David's fortitude in the face-off with the giant. Their opposite responses illustrate a substantial difference between those two men.

First, look at the response of the army under Saul's command: "As soon as the Israelite army saw [Goliath], they began to run away in fright" (17:24). Remember, King Saul is commander in chief of the Israelite army. Those soldiers take their cues from their leader. Where does he lead them? Saul is cowering in his tent, so his troops do the same. Why? Because they judge the situation by outward appearances, just as they had judged Saul.

Now look at David's response. He arrives on the battlefield to check on his older brothers and to bring them food (see 1 Samuel 17:12-15). The Israelite soldiers tell him about the king's huge reward for anyone who would kill the giant (see verse 25). David's response is immediate. No hemming and hawing, no lengthy strategizing. He says to King Saul, "Don't worry about this Philistine. . . . I'll go fight him!" (verse 32).

In reply to David's confidence, Saul says, "Don't be ridiculous! . . . There's no way you can fight this Philistine and possibly win! You're only a boy, and he's been a man of war since his youth" (17:33). These are the words of fear in the face of a giant. Saul—and the whole army of Israel with him—is looking only at the outward appearance.

In sharp contrast, David's next words reveal the source of his confidence. These aren't the words of braggadocio or adolescent folly.

These are words of firm conviction based on faith in the promises, provision, and protection of Almighty God:

> "I have been taking care of my father's sheep and goats," he said. "When a lion or a bear comes to steal a lamb from the flock, I go after it with a club and rescue the lamb from its mouth. If the animal turns on me, I catch it by the jaw and club it to death. I have done this to both lions and bears, and I'll do it to this pagan Philistine, too, for he has defied the armies of the living God! The LORD who rescued me from the claws of the lion and the bear will rescue me from this Philistine!"
>
> I SAMUEL 17:34-37

Though David's résumé doesn't list any battlefield experience, his portfolio as a shepherd includes plenty of real-world, life-and-death combat expertise—with lions and bears, no less! But David isn't depending simply on his skill in clubbing four-footed predators. His confidence is in the living God. Just as He rescued David from the most dangerous beasts of the field, He can rescue David from a giant named Goliath.

David has something else to rely on—the promise of future kingship as relayed by the prophet Samuel. Remember, David has been anointed as the next king of Israel. If he dies on the battlefield, God's promise will be nullified.

David's theology is too sound to believe God's promises can be broken.

Especially by a boastful, pagan enemy of Israel.

MIRACLE OR MERE HYPE?

Sometimes people talk about the showdown between David and Goliath as a miracle. Though we see God's providential protection and provision all over this story, there's nothing here we could properly call miraculous. David doesn't raise his staff and call lightning down from heaven. He doesn't strike the ground and open a crevice in the valley of Elah to swallow up Goliath. He doesn't pray for ten thousand angels to swoop down and slaughter the Philistine army. No, we see nothing overtly miraculous in this account.

What we do see is a refusal to accept that people and circumstances are what they appear to be on the surface. We see David sticking with his own tried-and-true methods of warfare. And we even see hints in the text that Goliath isn't as formidable an opponent as he is hyped up to be.

In the end, Goliath isn't some half-god/half-man titan. He is a mere human, like you and me. He has his weaknesses, even if they are hidden behind a veneer of Philistine frenzy.

At this point, let me hit pause on the narrative and make a few comments on ancient warfare as well as the intriguing clues about Goliath—clues I think David himself would have noticed.

A Few Insights into Ancient Warfare

Armies of the time would have been made up of a variety of troop units such as a cavalry, a chariot corps, and an infantry. The infantrymen were divided by the types of weapons they used. Short-range actions involved swords, clubs, or other lethal weapons for hand-to-hand combat. Midrange weapons included javelins and spears. And for long-range volleys, troops used bows and slings.[2]

Based on David's words, Goliath wielded a "sword, spear, and javelin" (1 Samuel 17:45), which would seem to place him in the company of the short- to midrange soldiers. However, the fact that he had a shield bearer (see verses 7 and 41) points us in a different direction. Archers and slingers needed shield bearers because their own implements of warfare required both hands. Infantrymen would carry their own shields because they needed to fend off the blows of enemies in their up-close-and-personal clashes. So, Goliath is presented as a towering super-soldier filling every role, like a one-man army.

To me, this all reeks of theatrics. Sure, Goliath may have been skilled in every kind of warfare. It's possible. But it's also possible the Philistines took an oversized oaf, decked him out in every type of weapon, then paraded him out at the front of their troops to scare the daylights out of their enemies. For this showmanship to work, Goliath didn't actually need to be an undefeated champion; the Israelite army just needed to believe he was.

Maybe the *real* Goliath didn't live up to the *hyped* Goliath. As we examine the account even more closely, we see other oddities that point in this direction. But before we look at the giant's hidden weaknesses, let's turn our attention to David for a moment.

When King Saul accepts the lad's offer to do battle with Goliath, he tries to outfit him with his own armor and shield—to enlist him, as it were, in the ranks of the close-combat infantry (see 1 Samuel 17:38-39). David's response is classic: "I can't go in these. . . . I'm not used to them" (verse 39). Instead, David strips off the helmet and coat of mail, selects five stones from a stream, and heads across the valley with his staff and sling. That was all he needed.

David was a slinger. Slingers were like snipers. They traveled lean and light. They wore no armor. Their weapon was a leather pouch called a "hand" with two long strands of leather or rope on each side. The pouch held the projectile—usually a stone or metal shot—launched by swinging the sling in a circle, building up speed, and releasing it at a high velocity. The sling was a devastating weapon. An expert slinger could hit a target up to 200 yards away—twice the length of a football field. One scholar even suggests David had attached his sling to the end of his staff to increase the speed and force of the blow.[3]

After investigating the use of the ancient sling, estimating likely velocity of a stone upon release, and calculating the speed on impact, historian Robert Dohrenwend argues, "These values give us an impact velocity of 127 feet per second . . . and an impact momentum of 0.52 lbsec [pound per second] . . . which is about that of a .38 Special revolver."[4] He then concludes: "Goliath had just as much chance against David as any Bronze Age warrior with a sword would have had against an adolescent armed with a .45 automatic pistol."[5]

If you doubt the potential power of an ancient sling, I suggest you squat behind home plate during a major league baseball game just as the pitcher's winding up.[6] Or stand between the tee and the green as a professional golfer is about to swing. Now imagine they're both aiming at your head. I don't know anybody who would put themselves in either of those positions without fearing for their lives.

Put simply, to a skilled slinger like David, the average infantryman was a sitting duck, weighed down with thick armor and heavy weapons.[7] Add Goliath's two more feet of height and his body weight, and his intimidating size becomes more of a liability than an advantage.

When it comes to giants, as the saying goes, "The bigger they are, the harder they fall."

Goliath's Hidden Weakness

I've already suggested the possibility that Goliath of Gath may have been more of an intimidating mascot than an invincible warrior. Not that he wasn't a force to be reckoned with or that just anybody could have bowled him over. But I've come to believe he was more smoke than fire, more hype than substance. Consider some of these often-overlooked clues in the text:[8]

1. First, I mentioned that Goliath came into the valley with a shield bearer, but Goliath wasn't an archer. Why would an infantryman the size of Goliath even need a shield bearer? Why wouldn't he carry the shield himself—sword in one hand, shield in the other? *Could it be his shield bearer played another role?*

2. Second, the giant's own comments are strange. Instead of going out to meet David on the field of battle, he beckons David to come to him: "Come over here, and I'll give your flesh to the birds and wild animals!" (1 Samuel 17:44). Why didn't Goliath rush out against David? He was the larger of the two. Why would he ask a slinger to come closer? That would be like asking a man with a .45-caliber gun to narrow the distance and improve his aim. *Unless, of course, Goliath couldn't see that David had a sling.*

3. Third, I notice something unusual about Goliath's taunt of David: "Am I a dog, that you come to me with sticks?"

(1 Samuel 17:43, NASB). Though some paraphrastic translations have Goliath uttering the more accurate "stick" because David had only a single staff (verse 40), I think the plural "sticks" is important. *Could it be that Goliath saw more than one stick, even though David carried only one?*

All these considerations have led some to conclude that Goliath had a hidden weakness. One that was concealed from those who judge only by outward appearances. One that wouldn't have been obvious to average-sized men looking at Goliath through the tainted pane of fear. But to somebody observant, willing to see beyond the facade, Goliath seems to have been plagued by a weakness waiting to be exploited.

Goliath's actions and words suggest he may have been suffering from a condition called acromegaly. The world-famous Mayo Clinic defines this disease as "a hormonal disorder that develops when your pituitary gland produces too much growth hormone during adulthood."[9] Often caused by a tumor of the pituitary gland, it can result in a condition called "gigantism," leading not only to an enlargement of bones, hands, feet, and facial features, but also to extreme height in adulthood. Another common problem caused by large pituitary tumors is the compression of surrounding structures in the head, including the optic nerves. This in turn can lead to blurred vision, loss of peripheral vision, and even blindness.[10]

Did Goliath actually suffer from acromegaly and gigantism? The biblical evidence seems to point in that direction. Ironically, then, the very same condition that may have led to Goliath's perceived strength—his menacing, monstrous form—may also have led to an inability to see much farther than a few meters directly in front of him.[11] Maybe this is why he (1) needed a shield bearer to carry out his duties like a service animal, (2) thought David had "sticks," and (3) had to beckon David to step into his space to fight.

There's a lesson in all this. Don't go by what you see on the surface.[12] All that Saul and the Israelites saw was a giant. Isn't that the way you and I tend to react? We hear frightening news or face an overwhelming obstacle, and our initial response is to size up the situation, turn heel, and fearfully flee. But the encounter with Goliath reminds us that people and problems that appear powerful and menacing aren't always what they seem to be.

I like to think David was able to put the pieces together and recognize weaknesses that nobody else had eyes to see. Instead of running away from Goliath, David ran toward him with confidence. By the time the bleary-eyed giant of Gath was able to see his opponent clearly, it was too late.

With the force of a .38 Special, David's single smooth stone struck its mark. Goliath went tumbling down, and David finished him off with the giant's own sword.

NAMING YOUR GIANTS

David's giant was named Goliath of Gath.

But what are the names of your giants?

Many face giants on the domestic front. Perhaps you have experienced the sadness, anger, and even shame that come with the specter of divorce; it can feel overwhelming at times. Or maybe your giant is a wandering son or daughter. The death of a parent, a spouse, or even a child is a loss that looms over you, casting its cold shadow on everything you do. Your giant could be a sick loved one dangling on a filament between life and death; you may be exhausted from caring for that person. You may be tending to a loved one with a disability or, perhaps, with Alzheimer's. These giants on the home front may tempt you to close the drapes and hide away, like King Saul cowering in his tent. I know the feeling. Over the years, Cynthia and I have faced all of these heartaches in our immediate and extended family—and have counseled countless others who had trouble seeing beyond them.

Many people face personal giants, such as severe, debilitating health conditions. Maybe you're distracted by a lawsuit or facing eviction from your home. Or perhaps you are coping with the consequences of poor decisions in the distant past; the domino effect of those decisions may feel like it could ruin your life. Maybe the giant you're facing is depression, anxiety, loneliness, or just the melancholy reality of growing older and feeling useless. If retirement isn't what you thought it would be, your giant may be regret or a gnawing, numbing boredom. Whatever your giant, it may seem small and silly to some people, but for you, it's a formidable enemy as petrifying as David's warrior from Gath.

Many today are dealing with financial giants. Maybe you're collapsing under a load of debt. You lost your job and can't find a new one. The bills are mounting. Perhaps your business went belly up. Or an investment tanked. Or you've been struck by sudden medical expenses or car repairs. Maybe you're in such severe financial straits that you're considering bankruptcy, which means you'll be coping with regret, disillusionment, embarrassment. You may have even considered suicide. Financial giants can make us want to run and hide, or to pretend there is no problem. All the while the monster of the valley seems to grow bigger and shout louder.

How about spiritual giants? Are you running from doubts? Wrestling with unbelief? Has your relationship with God and fellow believers cooled to room temperature while the guilt and shame keep taunting you? Maybe you have been defeated in your struggle with the pull of the flesh toward the allurements of the world and the temptations of the devil. You may feel spiritually and morally depleted, beaten up by church conflicts, worn down by a culture at war with Christianity. Is the pressure mounting, urging you to compromise your convictions? Those spiritual giants can be worse than anything in the domestic, personal, or financial realm. When our faith is attacked, it's easy to panic.

Though you're not armed with a sling and facing a menacing nine-foot-plus warrior on the battlefield, God has outfitted you with everything necessary for victory against the giants you're facing today (see 2 Peter 1:3). He has equipped you with the ever-powerful Spirit of God and all the necessary wisdom, character, virtue, and perseverance only He can give. You're equipped with the One who has never known intimidation or defeat. In fact, He lives within you (see 1 John 4:4). And because He's not a Spirit of fear but of power (see 2 Timothy 1:7), He can motivate you to get out of your tent of fear and confront whatever giants are in your path.

SLAYING YOUR GIANTS

What are you going to do about the giants around you?

Let me suggest a few strategies for victory based on David's response to Goliath.

1. **Don't listen to the voices telling you what can't be done.**
   Remember Saul's words to David when he heard the lad was
   going to deal with the giant (see 1 Samuel 17:33)?

   - "Don't be ridiculous!"
   - "There's no way!"
   - "You can't possibly win!"
   - "You're only a boy!"
   - "He's been a warrior since his youth!"

   Whenever we're facing a giant, we have to cut through a
   crowd of voices telling us all the reasons that the obstacle is
   unpassable, the challenge is unbeatable, or the bond is unbreak-
   able. Often, the voice is in our own heads. Sometimes it comes
   from people we love and respect. Other times it comes from
   opponents who want to see us living in defeat (like *they* are). If
   David had agreed with everything Saul said, Goliath would have
   continued unvanquished. If we listen to those voices telling us
   what can't be done, we've lost the battle even before it's begun.

2. **Remember how God strengthened you in the past.** In
   response to Saul's negative, pessimistic, and cynical appraisal,
   David pointed out how God had delivered him from
   situations just as bad—if not worse. David had defended
   helpless lambs against lions and bears, fighting them off
   with his hands and a club (see 1 Samuel 17:34-35). Then
   David drew a conclusion for Saul. If God gave him victory
   over animals to save his sheep, He would do the same with
   Goliath to save Israel: "The LORD who rescued me from

the claws of the lion and the bear will rescue me from this Philistine!" (verse 37).

I'm sure you have your own "lion and bear" stories. How God fought for you in the past. How He delivered you from your trials and struggles, enemies and opponents. Don't forget those stories. Tell them to yourself regularly. Tell them to your kids and grandkids. Call them to mind. They'll strengthen your own faith for today and also empower others to press on.

3. **Keep your theology straight.** Remember David's victory mantra? "This is the LORD's battle . . ." (1 Samuel 17:47). But even with this knowledge, in the face of a daunting threat David avoided two extremes—either sitting back passively waiting for God to act with no human contribution at all . . . or relying on his own strength and smarts to save himself.

Instead, David recognized that God's sovereignty doesn't undo personal responsibility; nor does personal action negate God's provision. On the one hand, David faced the giant with confident resolve:

- "I'll go fight him!" (1 Samuel 17:32)
- "I'll do it." (verse 36)
- "I will kill you and cut off your head." (verse 46)

On the other hand, he rested all his confidence on God:

- "The LORD . . . will rescue me." (verse 37)
- "Today the LORD will conquer you." (verse 46)
- "This is the LORD's battle." (verse 47)

Of course, these aren't opposing perspectives. The two hands work together. These two truths—God's sovereignty and our active participation—balance each other. And when your theology is balanced, so is your life. When you understand that God most often works in and through us, not apart from and in spite of us, your perspective is clear. When it gets fuzzy, you start doubting, running scared, and holding back.

In light of these truths, what are you going to do when the giants of life attack?

Let me speak from my lifetime of experience. You can't beat walking by faith. You can't beat stepping into the battle in the strength of the Lord. You can't beat ignoring the vocal majority who give you bad advice. Don't get swept up by the voice of the crowd.

Instead of hiding out in a tent of fear and excuses, gather your stones of faith, cross your own valley of Elah—and watch God work within you to slay the giant and lead you to victory.

CHAPTER 8

WHEN THORNS RIP OUR PRIDE

God's Wisdom When Your Pain Comes to Produce Growth

WE OFTEN CALL GOD THE GREAT PHYSICIAN—and He certainly is. We've already seen in chapter 3 that God can—and does—heal our bodies from physical illnesses according to His will and by His own means. Yet, His number one priority is *spiritual* health and healing. We know this because as uncomfortable as it may be to accept, God sometimes permits physical pain and suffering to bring about spiritual transformation and moral correction.

I've said it before, but it needs to be repeated. In the hands of the Great Physician, *there's purpose in pain.* As with a scalpel in the hands of a surgeon, God's purpose in pain is to heal, not to harm. As C. S. Lewis put it plainly years ago, pain "plants the flag of truth within the fortress of a rebel soul."[1]

We need to remember something else, too. We're never alone

in our pain. Our Great Physician is right there with us. His presence makes all the difference. God is relentlessly at work within us. If we're teachable, He shapes and molds us like soft lumps of clay. If we're resistant to His instruction, He sometimes bends and hammers at us like malleable sheets of metal. And if we're hardened against His discipline, He chisels and sculpts us like hard blocks of marble.

The Great Physician never runs out of treatments for our sin-sickness, regardless of its specific symptoms. He often uses unpleasant and painful circumstances on our road to spiritual fitness. He teaches us trust by reminding us how helpless we are. He teaches us patience by making us wait for what we want. He teaches us obedience by allowing us to experience the consequences of sin. He teaches us wisdom by allowing us to fail and make mistakes.

And He teaches us humility by sending thorns that rip away our pride.

THE PROBLEM WITH PRIDE

In my experience, the number one obstacle to finishing well in Christian life and ministry is not sexual immorality or unbridled greed. Those obvious candidates get all the press. We see images of shamed preachers, heads bowed low, implicated in sexual sins they had preached against for years. Or we see investigative journalists exposing a televangelist's private jet, fleet of sports cars, or several million-dollar homes.

Those head-turning and heartbreaking stories may make headlines, but the real enemy to finishing well often goes undivulged and unreported: *pride.* That insidious sin of the heart is the root of the more obvious fruits—envy, boasting, unteachability, arrogance, self-ish ambition, lust, and greed.

I've observed that pride is a particularly acute malady for three categories of people who have a disposition toward it: the highly intelligent, the greatly gifted, and the deeply religious. Genius, talent, and spirituality attract attention, laud, and applause. Pride is quick to take a bow. Yet this disease of pride can quickly turn into a condition that disfigures our character.

The book of Proverbs has plenty to say about pride and its disastrous effects. Note the outcome of pride in this handful of proverbs:

> Pride leads to disgrace, but with humility comes wisdom.
>
> PROVERBS 11:2

> Pride leads to conflict; those who take advice are wise.
>
> PROVERBS 13:10

> Pride goes before destruction, and haughtiness before a fall.
>
> PROVERBS 16:18

> Pride ends in humiliation, while humility brings honor.
>
> PROVERBS 29:23

No wonder "God opposes the proud but gives grace to the humble" (James 4:6; 1 Peter 5:5). If left unchecked, pride will bring utter ruin to our ministries, our families, and our lives.

In this mortal life, burdened by our sin nature and surrounded by temptations, no instant remedy completely cures the disease of pride.

It won't be cured until these sinful bodies are replaced by glorious bodies free from corruption. Yet God hasn't left us to suffer from the affliction of pride without treatment in this life.

But there's a catch. God's medicine for pride is a big pill to swallow.

If God despises anything in the realm of sin in our lives, it's pride. So, because He loves us and refuses to abandon us to our destructive sins, He applies what I've termed "thorn therapy." Put bluntly, it's God's preferred treatment to cut us down to size. To show you what I mean by this, let's consider the experience of the apostle Paul.

PAUL'S REASONS FOR PRIDE

We usually see artistic portrayals of Paul with a serene expression on his bearded face and sometimes a bright halo hovering over his head. His own words, though, set the record straight. They reveal a much deeper, more earthy reality. As we open the pages of his testimony, we learn he was once a proud, angry, and aggressive man—full of himself and overflowing with self-confidence. To use Paul mightily in the proclamation of the gospel to the Gentiles, God would have to knock him off his high horse and deal with those deep-seated blights on his character.

In several places in Paul's letters, we catch a glimpse of his own biography. If we tallied up the birthright and achievements that made Saul of Tarsus the person he was prior to meeting his Messiah, he would certainly have reason to boast from a human perspective. He writes:

I could have confidence in my own effort if anyone could. Indeed, if others have reason for confidence in their own efforts, I have even more!

I was circumcised when I was eight days old. I am a pure-blooded citizen of Israel and a member of the tribe of Benjamin—a real Hebrew if there ever was one! I was a member of the Pharisees, who demand the strictest obedience to the Jewish law. I was so zealous that I harshly persecuted the church. And as for righteousness, I obeyed the law without fault.

PHILIPPIANS 3:4-6

Beyond that, Paul's upbringing and education sweeten his CV. When testifying before a crowd of fellow Jews in Jerusalem, he says, "I am a Jew, born in Tarsus, a city in Cilicia, and I was brought up and educated here in Jerusalem under Gamaliel. As his student, I was carefully trained in our Jewish laws and customs. I became very zealous to honor God in everything I did, just like all of you today" (Acts 22:3). Not only was Paul born Jewish, he was also a Roman citizen by birth (see Acts 22:27-28).

If anybody has a pedigree to flex or privilege to flaunt, it's Saul of Tarsus. His high intelligence is paired with top schooling. His great giftedness borders on genius. And his religious zeal rivals that of any of the Jewish people.

In short, Paul has all the preconditions for a terminal case of pride.

Even after his sudden, shocking, and humbling conversion to Christ (see Acts 9), his incredible life experiences and eye-opening revelations would have stoked the fires of pride in anybody (see 2 Corinthians 11:21-33).

Deep into his apostolic ministry, in his most autobiographical letter, Paul unveils important details about his private world. Personal struggles. Frustrations with circumstances. Longings and disappointments. Pleading with God.

In 2 Corinthians, Paul reveals details we find nowhere else in all the New Testament. Chapter 12 of that insightful letter puts us in direct contact with Paul's own case of "thorn therapy" for his chronic disease of pride.

Paul may well have been regarded by his peers as brilliant, gifted, and a spiritual force to be reckoned with. It would be hard to argue with that view of him. After all, to this day—centuries after their writing—his words still stump scholars and provoke people to ponder profound truths. Paul's ministry certainly impacted not only his own generation but countless generations worldwide ever since.

Yet in the midst of that powerful ministry, Paul has much to learn about humility.

In fact, he says the powerful religious experiences that fueled his public ministry and affected his personal life *also fed his pride*.

Or at least they would have if God hadn't stepped in.

PAUL'S THORN THERAPY

In 2 Corinthians 12, Paul mentions a spiritual experience so intense that he can't make sense of it—and so exceptional that he isn't even allowed to describe it in detail. In his own words: "I was caught up to the third heaven fourteen years ago" (verse 2). He goes on, "I was caught up to paradise and heard things so astounding that they cannot be expressed in words, things no human is allowed to tell" (verse 4).

In the ecstasy of the overwhelming, he isn't sure if he was caught up bodily or if he had a kind of out-of-body journey into the spiritual realm (see 2 Corinthians 12:2-3). All he knows is that it happened: an invitation-only admission into the throne room of God.

One detail stands out to me. When Paul wrote 2 Corinthians, that experience was fourteen years old. As far as we know, Paul was reporting on it for the first time. I'm not sure I could name a single person who could keep their lips sealed on such an experience for so long—only to pull it out reluctantly to prove a point (see 2 Corinthians 12:1).

Contrast Paul's reaction with today's fortuitous "tourists" of heaven. They're often people who aren't very religious to start with. They claim to have had near-death experiences, seeing bright lights, angels, and the souls of departed loved ones, and they give remarkably detailed descriptions of God, Jesus, and heaven. I've also noticed the various accounts never seem to agree with each other! Those claims usually give rise to best-selling books, multinational marketing blitzes, and television or movie adaptations.

Not so with Paul. Instead, he follows up his glimpse of heaven with fourteen years of silence. He never tries to market his experience. Never publishes an account. Never once in the book of Acts do we see Paul owning his critics with a cocky "I've been to heaven" response. Nor does he casually introduce himself with "Hi, I'm Paul, I've seen the throne room of God."

Paul despised the thought of being put on a pedestal. I have no doubt he would cringe at the countless icons, paintings, and statues portraying him as "Saint Paul." He even has churches and cities named after him! Paul knew he was a mere mortal like you and me. And if ever the occasion arose in which his lofty spiritual experiences tempted him to exalt himself, God's thorn therapy ripped holes in his pride.

Immediately after the reluctant mention of his journey to paradise, Paul clues us in on the method God used to keep him from strutting around like a Christian hotshot. Instead of following his natural, fallen inclination to boast about that event, he chooses to boast about the weak condition—brought on by God himself—that took him down a peg.

Paul says, "To keep me from becoming proud, I was given a thorn in my flesh, a messenger from Satan to torment me and keep me from becoming proud" (2 Corinthians 12:7). Most likely your eyes focused on the words "thorn in my flesh" or "messenger from Satan." Certainly, those phrases deserve our attention. I'll get to them. But you might have missed the fact that Paul mentions the reason for the thorn not once but *twice*: to "keep me from becoming proud."

That's Paul's focus. And it should be ours, too.

God takes the sin of pride very seriously.

Each May, at the end of the academic year at Dallas Seminary, the handful of top preachers of the senior class get a turn in the pulpit of Chafer Chapel. One year a talented young man preached on the passage in John 13 in which Jesus washed His disciples' feet. Talk about humility! It's hard to beat Jesus' example.

After a compelling exposition of that simple text, the young senior-class preacher leaned low into the microphone, looked across the faces in that auditorium, and asked his fellow students, "Do you want to have a great ministry—or do you just want to be great?"

The packed chapel went silent. Nobody blinked.

Though the question was directed toward the students, it hit everybody hard—from junior faculty to seminary president. I'll never forget that question. I doubt that anyone who heard it will.

With that single challenge, he captured the crucial issue: greatness. Let us seek greatness not as the world defines it but according to the example of Christ. A greatness achieved not by flexing worldly power but by breaking earthly pride.

THE PUZZLING THORN IN THE FLESH

Now to the question you're itching to know the answer to: What's this thorn Paul is talking about? Nobody interprets the "thorn in my flesh" as a literal thorn. But to what, exactly, does this vivid metaphor point? For centuries, commentators have speculated about what it represents.[2]

Some have suggested that it signifies spiritual temptations. Perhaps Paul began to doubt what he had observed with his own eyes or heard with his own ears, like seeing the resurrected Jesus or being snatched up into heaven. How easy it would have been to doubt his own senses when faced with arrest, torture, and execution.

Others have suggested the thorn refers to the range of sufferings Paul described in 2 Corinthians 11. He had endured trials, beatings, imprisonment, sleepless nights, abandonment, and betrayal. Such experiences would have left him brutalized, beleaguered, and certainly humbled.

Some commentators have thought that maybe Paul struggled with a sexual temptation he had to constantly battle to keep under control. After all, the celibate life to which he was called (see 1 Corinthians 7:7) isn't always easy. Perhaps every time he felt pride pining for the spotlight, his carnal desires reminded him he was a sinner like the rest of us.

Maybe the thorn was a physical handicap—a disfigurement, a chronic disease, severe migraines, malarial fevers, or even a speech impediment.

Or some think the thorn might have been a literal "messenger of Satan." Was Paul afflicted by demonic oppression? I think that's unlikely. It's more likely that he uses the phrase "messenger of Satan" as an analogy. That is, Paul is probably saying, "This thing torments me so much it's like . . . like . . . a thorn lodged in my flesh . . . or . . . a demon assaulting me day and night!"

So many theories. And all of them seem plausible. So, what was his affliction?

The word translated "thorn" is the Greek *skolops*. Say that out loud. It just sounds nasty, doesn't it? If somebody told you they had a chronic case of skolops, you'd probably keep your distance. But the term itself simply refers to anything pointed—like a stake, a thorn, or a splinter.[3] In Paul's case, it evidently caused chronic pain, discomfort, or frustration.

We shouldn't be dogmatic about what the thorn is, because Scripture never states it clearly. But I tend to think Paul was suffering from failing eyesight. Look at what he says in Galatians 4:15: "I am sure you would have taken out your own eyes and given them to me if it had been possible." At the end of the letter, Paul remarks, "NOTICE WHAT LARGE LETTERS I USE AS I WRITE THESE CLOSING WORDS IN MY OWN HANDWRITING" (6:11). Could it be that he had to rely on secretaries and scribes to read and write for him because he could barely see? If so, I could certainly relate to his frustration. Due to my own eye problems, I had to rely for a time on a magnifying glass and bright lights to be able to see. If

Paul had glaucoma or cataracts, it would certainly explain some of his struggles.

We may never know. What we do know is this thorn assaulted Paul like an implacable demon repeatedly attacking him.

But why? Why would God use such a method to pummel Paul's pride? Why such a devastating, relentless pain?

WHEN OUR PLEADING GOES UNANSWERED

Regardless of the specific meaning of Paul's thorn, we should think differently about Paul than how he is often portrayed. Not as a tall, bold statue of marble affixed to a high pedestal but as a man hunched over, eyes to the ground, nursing a physical ailment. As he preached the gospel, he may have winced in pain. As he dictated the inspired words of his letters, he likely needed to pause in his discomfort or lie down to regain his strength from time to time.

Remember this as you read his words. Remember that these aren't the words of a tenured theologian speculating about the world from an overstuffed chair in his comfortable office. These words are forged on the anvil of pain. Right up to the day of his death, Paul probably labored through incessant physical suffering or frustration.

How about you? Are you struggling with chronic pain? Are you burdened by a physical, mental, or emotional challenge? Have you begged the Lord repeatedly to take it away? Pleaded with Him? Bargained? Asked Him over and over, "Why, God?" You're not alone. You have a companion in Paul.

Paul begged the Lord to take away his thorn. Not once. Not twice. *Three times.* The word translated "begged" (see 2 Corinthians 12:8) implies much more than a casual "ask." Paul implored, entreated, strongly urged God to action, pleading with Him to come to his aid.[4] Not the "God, give me a parking space" kind of prayer people thoughtlessly toss up to the sky, but the fall-on-your-face, groan-in-agony, sweat-like-blood kind of prayer Jesus repeated three times in the garden of Gethsemane (see Matthew 26:36-46).

God's answer?

Despite Paul's repeated, heart-wrenching pleas, the Lord never freed Paul of his pain as far as we are told in Scripture. Why not? Because God had a purpose in the pain.

God didn't just drop an emphatic "NO!" on Paul's prayers. Instead, He revealed the underlying reason for the thorn in the flesh: to keep Paul from proudly promoting himself among his peers and to prevent him from strutting around like a celebrity among his disciples. Also, with the explanation came words of comfort and encouragement: "My grace is all you need. My power works best in weakness" (2 Corinthians 12:9).

I think both the reasons for the pain and the reassurance amid the pain apply to us today. I have no reason to think God has stopped using thorn therapy to treat the disease of pride. In fact, my personal experience and decades of observing how God works in the lives of others strengthen this conviction.

The thorns God allows in our lives humble us. Especially if we're highly intelligent, greatly gifted, or deeply spiritual. When we're tempted to rouse the applause of an adoring public, the thorns remind us that we, too, are in the flesh. We, too, are mere mortals. We, too, are weak and unworthy of the glory that belongs to God and God alone.

By sending Paul's thorn in the flesh, the Lord taught the apostle that His power is made perfect through the weaknesses of His servants. We're now getting a glimpse of paradoxical power—our weakness is God's strength. Martin Luther comments on this paradox: "It is a strange sort of strength which is weak and by its weakness grows stronger. Who ever heard of weak strength? Or more absurd still, that strength is increased by weakness?"[5]

Luther was right. In most people's minds, it's a contradiction to have strength through weakness. You'll never read about it in *Fortune* magazine. You'll never hear a TED talk on it or read a how-to book on success that discusses the key to power through weakness. You don't hear about it from the world's "high places." Regrettably, it's not even a given among fellow pastors and ministry leaders.

What will it take to convince us that in God's spiritual economy, pride comes before a fall, the last will be first, and weakness is spiritually powerful? It sometimes takes a lifetime of constant reminders in the form of thorn therapy.

How I wish we displayed this idea of strength in weakness better!

The apostle Paul describes it here in the Lord's words: "My grace is all you need" (2 Corinthians 12:9). I love those six words. I can't tell you how many times they have ministered to me in the ditches of pain and the back alleys of despair. When we don't get relief from the thorns, His grace ministers to us, comforts us, and strengthens us. And because of that, we don't quit. We don't give up. We don't wobble in our theology. We don't waffle in our faith in a good, loving, all-powerful, all-wise God. Because in our weakness manifested in the flesh, *His grace is all we need.*

HARD-TO-HEAR TRUTH

Suffering is a delicate subject. It's not easy to address because I realize that you may have dwelled in a depth of suffering I've never known. Yes, my family and I have had our bouts with both "come and go" and "come and stay" challenges. Chronic neck pain, migraines, eye problems—the typical things we deal with as we overripen in these frail bodies of flesh and bone.

But in no way do I want to give the impression that I'm a model of how to go through suffering. To be honest with you, I fail in my responses to adversity as much as anybody. It's a lot easier to preach on it or write about it than to live it consistently. Along with the pity parties I throw for myself once in a while, my heart is occasionally broken, and my spirit sometimes takes a tumble.

Now, I'm admitting all this because I know you'll probably say that's your experience too. Few people would have stopped at Paul's three desperate pleas to God for relief from his chronic condition. Let's be honest. When it becomes clear God is not going to take our suffering away, we lower our gaze from Him and instead spill our guts to people around us.

So, let me put my pastor's badge on again and preach a hard word we all need to hear—including me. It's a difficult word to hear. In fact, it's even tough to say. But it's true. What is that word?

We need to quit complaining about our pain.

We need to stop begging over and over for relief. God has heard your prayers. He knows your desires. If He wants to pluck that thorn from your flesh, He'll do it.

But what if He doesn't?

Our incessant obsessing over our pain may be short-circuiting what God is trying to teach us. When we camp on all the things *we can't* do, we're unable to see the things *God can* do through us.

Instead of complaining endlessly, we need to lift our eyes to Him. To find His strength in our weakness. To lean into His sustaining grace. We need to say often, "His grace is all I need."

Like you, I'm weak. I struggle. I'm vulnerable. I suffer from all the ailments of being mortal. But I often repeat His words: "My grace is all you need."

Look at the difference this truth made in Paul's life. When he recognized God's sustaining grace, He ceased his repeated pleading for relief and accepted what God was doing not *to* him but *for* him: "That's why I take pleasure in my weaknesses, and in the insults, hardships, persecutions, and troubles that I suffer for Christ. For when I am weak, then I am strong" (2 Corinthians 12:10).

Insults didn't offend Paul. Hardships didn't discourage him. Persecutions didn't shatter him. Troubles didn't crush him. When Paul was at his weakest, God was at His strongest. Through His thorn therapy, God put Paul's pride in time-out.

THE FATHER KNOWS BEST

Some of the most difficult—and most vital—lessons I've learned in life are simple and obvious—*but so hard to reconcile with our everyday experiences.*

God is no dummy.
God knows us.
God never goofs up.

God never says, "Whoops! Messed that one up! I guess I should have answered Chuck's prayer like he asked. Well, maybe I'll get it right next time."

No. We can rest all our confidence in the fact that God the Father knows best. He knows what to give us, what to keep from us, and how much we can handle as He seeks to accomplish His purpose of keeping us humbly dependent on Him.

The Lord has specific trials with our name on them. They're designed for us, arranged with our weaknesses and maturity level in mind. He bears down and doesn't let up. Yet He's always in control, making sure the trials are no more and no less than we need.

Yes, we groan and weep. But we also learn and grow.

Understandably, our common reaction to thorn therapy is resistance. Sometimes even resentment. But how much better would it be for you and me if we were to open the doors of our hearts when God's perfectly timed trials come knocking?

What Paul says about his own pride-pummeling thorn therapy isn't easy to hear. I'm sure as Paul penned the litany of pain, mistreatment, and hardship he had endured during his ministry (see 2 Corinthians 11:23-28), the memories made him wince. Scars that deep never fully heal.

For the highly intelligent, greatly gifted, and deeply religious, pride is often the major roadblock in the path to maturity. But the Lord uses painful events and chronic suffering to mold us and fashion us into the image of His Son.

At times, God will use thorn therapy to make you aware of attitudes and behaviors in your own life that need to be changed. It may seem like He's crushing you, but in reality He's curing you. It may feel like He's harming you, but He's healing you. Let's be brutally honest: it may look like He hates you, but He loves you.

You may be there right now—sensing a little thorn therapy from the Father. And for the first time in your life, you may realize that there is a holy purpose in it all. He's calling you to attention and turning you away from yourself and toward His Son.

If your pain has brought you to your knees, I commend you to our loving Father. That's the best place to begin the rest of your life. I invite you to call out to Him. Tell Him that your fight is over, that you willingly surrender.

In utter and complete weakness, tell Him you've come to the end of your own resources. The crushing in this crucible has made you aware of your desperate need for hope, a hope that is found only in the Lord Jesus Christ.

Tell him this—say it aloud: "Your grace is enough for me."

CHAPTER 9

WHEN GOD'S DISCIPLINE STRIKES

God's Wisdom When You Need Correction

IN MY EXPERIENCE, God's people who have seen much affliction are immensely patient. They're usually wise and insightful. They seem to have just the right words—or the appropriate silence—at just the right moments. Many times, I've sat in hospital rooms beside older saints in the throes of suffering, and later I've left their rooms realizing they ministered more to me than I to them.

I've had the privilege of sitting at the feet of many such saints whose lives manifested the fruit of the Spirit. In each case, the image of Christ had been fashioned through the painful chipping away of everything that didn't conform to Him. I often didn't learn of the individuals' great hardships and personal suffering until later. All I knew was they were fine teachers through their attitudes, their words, and their actions—and I wanted to be like them.

Through the years, I learned the reason they were such good teachers: *they had been such good students.*

The training ground of life designed for God's children includes suffering. We've discussed this vital concept several times in previous chapters. Usually, this suffering comes because we live in mortal bodies in a fallen world. But often, the suffering comes as a direct result of the Lord's loving discipline in our lives.

In this lifelong training, the great Teacher knows you thoroughly and loves you unconditionally. You can trust Him. You can trust His process. If you stick with it, you'll eventually see signs that you're growing. You'll grasp principles you never understood before. You'll gain insight into yourself and others. You'll go deeper into the truths of God.

But the process will be punctuated with pain.

TWO KINDS OF DISCIPLINE

This is a good time to pause and think about two kinds of discipline the Lord uses in life's training ground. Let's call them *constructive discipline* and *corrective discipline*. Sometimes they are called positive discipline and negative discipline, but that gives the wrong impression. Both constructive and corrective discipline are positive in their outcome. Both can involve pain. And both have the same end in mind—our growth toward maturity.

The Benefits of Constructive Discipline

In the physical realm, *constructive* discipline promotes behaviors like engaging in effective study habits, committing to a rigorous workout routine, or maintaining an organized schedule. In the spiritual realm, it strengthens what we call spiritual disciplines, like reading our Bibles regularly, attending church, memorizing Scripture, and staying engaged in a nurturing small group. These activities reinforce what is true and teach us by word and by example to do what's right.

When I think of constructive discipline, I think of the late Tom Landry, head coach of the Dallas Cowboys from 1960 to 1988. I had the great privilege of getting to know him when he served on the Dallas Theological Seminary Board of Incorporate Members. A humble man of quiet strength, he modeled constructive discipline as well as anyone I've ever known personally.

On one occasion, I asked him how he was able to forge a team out of a bunch of strong-willed, independent individuals, so that they won so often during his twenty-nine seasons as their coach. He smiled as he responded. To this day his answer is fresh in my mind: "The key is discipline. And what's that? It's to get men to do what they don't want to do in order to achieve what they've always wanted to accomplish in their lives." Yes, Coach Landry worked his team hard. He drilled them mercilessly. But by all accounts, he did it with great love and respect. His primary goal was to build up and equip.

The Benefits of Corrective Discipline

When I think of *corrective* discipline, my mind goes back to the early weeks of Marine Corps boot camp. I must have heard our drill instructor shout the words "I'm going to cut you down to size!" dozens of times. That man had his work cut out for him. His goal was to take a ragtag bunch of young men from every conceivable background and shred their self-sufficient arrogance, independent spirits, and rebellious tendencies. His relentless corrective discipline worked. Any indifference toward authority was replaced by a firm commitment to do only as we were told, regardless of the situation.

Of course, constructive discipline involves correction of mistakes and errors as well. And corrective discipline removes bad attitudes and behaviors to make way for the good. These two types of discipline are always meant to work together, like two hands fashioning a lump of clay on a potter's wheel. In fact, after several weeks of cutting us new recruits down to size (which was about six inches tall), the US Marine Corps built us up bigger and stronger than we had ever been in all our lives. With one hand they tore us down, with the other they put us back together. Almost without realizing it, while learning to submit ourselves to the commands of the leader, we ultimately found ourselves physically fit, emotionally stirred, and mentally ready for whatever conflict might come our way, even the harsh reality of facing a fierce enemy in combat.

As we continue exploring the ins and outs of God's training ground, we'll focus mostly on corrective discipline. We'll see that God uses personal pain to correct sinful attitudes and actions in us, His children. He also uses the example of discipline experienced by others to warn us about the consequences of sin.

REMEMBER THE WARNINGS

Warning signs are everywhere. Usually brief and to the point, they communicate their clear meanings in just a few words:

WARNING: DO NOT ENTER
WARNING: HIGH VOLTAGE
WARNING: STRONG CURRENTS

We encounter warning signs several times a day. They turn us away from harm and lead us toward safety.

Another kind of warning comes not by reading a sign but by looking backward at history. Such lessons inform our present and help us take better steps into our future. By seeing how people of the past suffered after a certain course of action, we're cautioned not to follow the same path.

The word *warning* isn't included at the beginning of 1 Corinthians 10, but it could have been. In the first thirteen verses of that chapter, Paul points readers of his day back to people and events of the past that serve as warnings for us today as well. The episodes he recounts aren't snapshots from glorious years of blessing and success meant to encourage imitation. Rather, Paul's descriptions of rebellion and discipline are meant to alert us to the consequences of sin among God's people.

Paul begins his warnings from the past with a call to attention: "I don't want you to forget, dear brothers and sisters, about our ancestors in the wilderness long ago" (1 Corinthians 10:1).

Having turned the Corinthians' heads back to consider the Hebrew people during their long journey in the wilderness, Paul writes the words "all of them," not once or twice, but five specific times in the first four verses. He reminds them of the astonishing privileges the Israelites experienced in their deliverance from Egypt following the Exodus.

- "All of them were guided by a cloud that moved."
  (1 Corinthians 10:1)
- "All of them walked through the sea on dry ground." (10:1)
- "All of them were baptized as followers of Moses." (10:2)
- "All of them ate the same spiritual food." (10:3)
- "All of them drank the same spiritual water." (10:4)

These rapid-fire reminders serve two purposes for Paul. First, they rehearse the miraculous ways in which God provided for His people during their deliverance from Egypt. Any of his readers with some knowledge of the Old Testament book of Exodus would have been able to fill in the details. The Israelites passed under the cloud, which represented the presence of the Holy Spirit among the Israelites (see Exodus 13:21). They also passed through the Red Sea in that miraculous deliverance from their enemies (14:21-22). Then, in a sense, the Hebrew people were "baptized" into Moses—that is, fully associated with the deliverer God used to redeem them from slavery in Egypt (14:31). Finally, together they partook of the food and drink God miraculously provided for them in the wilderness (16:4-36). These reminders emphasize the awe-inspiring power of God and His abundant love for His people.

Second, these reminders serve as "types"—foreshadowing pictures—of the Corinthians' own experiences of spiritual redemption in Christ. They had experienced the indwelling of the Holy Spirit (see 1 Corinthians 3:16). They had passed through the waters of baptism, marking their deliverance from bondage to sin (1:13-15). They had been baptized into Christ as head of the Church by the baptism of the Holy Spirit (12:13). And they had partaken of the Lord's Supper as a mark of their spiritual fellowship with Christ and one another (10:16-17).

The miraculous blessings of physical deliverance for the Israelites were for *all of them*. By analogy, the miraculous blessings of spiritual deliverance for Christians are for *all believers*. Nobody is overlooked. Everybody "in Christ" is granted vast blessings—just as everybody "in Moses" found themselves on the other side of the Red Sea, safe and sound, under God's protection and provision.

Back to the Israelites. At first blush, those wilderness wanderings after their deliverance from Egypt sound like a cakewalk. If we stopped reading at verse 4, we might get the impression that their journey was a case study in prosperity, success, and one victory after another. You'd think that with such a barrage of constant blessings, the people of Israel would at least have stayed faithful. They would at least have sought to please the God who delivered them, right?

Wrong.

WARNINGS THAT STILL APPLY TODAY

After a rousing review of the blessings lavished upon the Israelites during their exodus from Egypt, Paul's retelling of the tale takes a dramatic turn. In the Greek text we see a word indicating a sharp contrast—*alla*, "but."

But what? "God was not pleased with most of them" (1 Corinthians 10:5).

Though all of the Israelites had been blessed, *most* of them failed.

Not just little mistakes like eating one too many flakes of manna or an occasional discontented sigh that earned a soft rebuke. Most of them failed monumentally.

And by "most," Paul really means *most*. Shockingly, out of the hundreds of thousands of Israelites rescued from their bondage in Egypt, only Moses, Joshua, and Caleb pleased God. The rest of the rebellious Hebrews were left scattered across the wilderness over the next forty years. One commentator captures the stark contrast between the blessings of verses 1 to 4 and the warning of verse 5: "All those bodies, sated with miraculous food and drink, strewing the soil of the desert!"[1]

At this point, Paul could have drawn a box in the margin of his papyrus with the word *warning!* The sobering image of God's discipline serves as a serious caution to all of us. In fact, Paul states directly, "These things happened as a warning to us" (1 Corinthians 10:6), and "These things happened to them as examples for us. They were written down to warn us who live at the end of the age" (verse 11).

That "us" includes you and me. From the time those events happened and were written down, they were meant to warn us and others. They remind us with vivid imagery that God will discipline even the children upon whom He has lavished His blessings.

But what is the warning for? What attitudes and actions warranted such harsh rebuke? Let's take a closer look at the warnings in 1 Corinthians 10:6-10—as relevant for us today as for the Corinthians in the first century.

Warning: Do Not Crave Evil Things!

Lusting after evil things is what fallen humans do best. Dissatisfaction, discontentment, and ingratitude led the Hebrews to long for the luxuries of Egypt (see Numbers 11:4-6). They had grown impatient with God's timing and the long journey (see 11:4). In the same way, how tempting it is for us to go back to our evil ways when following Christ introduces hardship and heartache!

Warning: Do Not Worship Idols!

At first glance, I find it unimaginable that, after being delivered from Egypt through such spectacular miracles as the splitting of the Red Sea, the Hebrews would fashion a golden calf and call it their God (see Exodus 32:4-6). Then I remember that the human heart is full of idolatry. Anything can become an idol for you and me, whether people, ideologies, institutions, or material possessions.

Warning: Do Not Engage in Sexual Immorality!

Within minutes, the Israelites' idolatry descended into a drunken orgy (Exodus 32:6-7). The general pattern of moral decline described in Romans 1:23-24 came to pass: "Instead of worshiping the glorious, ever-living God, they worshiped idols made to look like mere people and birds and animals and reptiles. So God abandoned them to do whatever shameful things their hearts desired. As a result, they did vile and degrading things with each other's bodies." I don't have to convince you that Paul's warning against sexual immorality is just as relevant in the twenty-first century as it was in the first. God's discipline for craving evil things, worshiping idols, and engaging in immorality fell hard: 23,000 Israelites died in one day (see 1 Corinthians 10:8). We would do well to take heed of how seriously God views our disobedience.

Warning: Do Not Put God to the Test!

Numbers 21:5 tells us that the Hebrews "began to speak against God and Moses. 'Why have you brought us out of Egypt to die here in the wilderness?' they complained. 'There is nothing to eat here and nothing to drink. And we hate this horrible manna!'" God's discipline for testing His faithfulness was immediate: "So the LORD sent poisonous snakes among the people, and many were bitten and died" (verse 6). God led them out of Egypt and promised to take care of them. In return, they doubted that He would follow through. How easy it is for us to do the same!

Warning: Do Not Grumble!

Finally, Paul reminds his readers that the Israelites grumbled against God's established leaders (see Numbers 16:41; 17:5, 10). Yes, baseless, relentless complaining about leaders is a serious matter. James 5:9 says, "Don't grumble about each other, brothers and sisters, or you will be judged." And Jude 1:16 tells us that false teachers are "grumblers and complainers, living only to satisfy their desires." In our day, grumbling is often given a pass. We may roll our eyes at complaining, but we don't take it seriously. At least not as seriously as God does. But it can rip apart families, churches, businesses—and entire nations. This is why God's discipline for grumbling hit hard: they "were destroyed by the angel of death" (1 Corinthians 10:10).

WHEN WE DESERVE DISCIPLINE

Impatience, impertinence, impiety, immorality—all of these build to a crescendo that ends with a booming crash—God's discipline. In the middle of the night, the Israelites find snakes crawling all around them. What a horrifying scene! Yet how fitting that God sends snakes against those who followed the temptations of the serpent, who were striking out with verbal insults, and who were spouting venomous complaints against God and Moses.

In the case of the Israelites, though, the discipline has its intended effect. The people "came to Moses and cried out, 'We have sinned by speaking against the LORD and against you. Pray that the LORD will take away the snakes'" (Numbers 21:7). The main purpose for the Lord's corrective discipline, which can be extremely painful at the time, is not ultimately to harm us but to heal us—to "cut us down to size." He allows such suffering in our lives to lead us not to ruin but to repentance.

At least this story ends well. After Moses prays for the people, the Lord instructs Moses to fashion a replica of the venomous snakes and hang it on a pole. The people merely have to look at the bronze serpent to be healed (Numbers 21:8-9).

But how had they gotten so cynical to begin with? Why were they so jaded? Simple: *they were spoiled and entitled.* Remember those amazing "all of them" experiences (1 Corinthians 10:1-4)? Those were unparalleled expressions of God's unearned grace and unmerited mercy. Yet after several weeks, months, and even years in that wilderness, the Israelites had come to believe that God's grace was their right. They convinced themselves that somehow they deserved those things—and more!

It's easy for us to look back at their gross ingratitude and to think we would have behaved differently. Think about it. They were in the wilderness for *forty years*! The glory of the original deliverance had begun to wane amid the daily grind. The luster of the miraculous exodus didn't shine as brightly after a couple decades of seemingly aimless meandering. The Law they had enthusiastically embraced had started to feel like a stale religious routine.

I often see this same kind of malaise in ministry. Sometime after the honeymoon, a newly married couple who were googly-eyed over each other start to grate on each other's nerves. A new church gathering buzzes with energy and excitement, but a few years later the "fresh and new" feels "old and worn." In my own roles as president and then chancellor at Dallas Seminary, I've often heard students talk about the excitement of the first few weeks of seminary. It's so engaging, inspiring, and exhilarating. They love what they're reading, love their professors, love their fellow students, and love being in chapel. Then, several years later at the end of their degree programs, many of those once bright-eyed seminarians can't wait to box up their books and never look at them again.

It's the same in the church. We come Sunday after Sunday. We take our seats. We sing the songs—the same songs we've been singing for years. We hear sermons from that same old preacher. We have to look at the backs of the same people sitting in the same places week after week.

And God help the visitor who comes early and sits in your seat!

It reminds me of something that happened when I was a little kid. My family went to the same church for years. My mom would hold my hand as we followed dad into the sanctuary each Sunday and sat in the same seats. They were *our* seats, after all.

One Sunday, the Swindoll family moseyed in as usual. We suddenly halted at the door, noticing the visitors—in *our* seats. I'll never forget that moment. My mom turned to my dad and said, "Well, Earl, what should we do?"

My dad frowned and said, "Well, Lovell, I think we should go home." And we did. Why? Because we were spoiled. We had grown comfortable. We had become selfish.

How easy it is to slip into such jaded cynicism!

And how loving when God sends His discipline to get our attention and correct our attitude.

A FATHER'S CORRECTION

From a purely human perspective, the examples of God's discipline of the Israelites may appear unjust, severe, vindictive—even spiteful. Yet the New Testament book of Hebrews sets the record straight and shines a heavenly light on our dim, earthly understanding of God's corrective discipline.

The fact is, as a loving father will discipline his son, our heavenly Father disciplines His children. The means He uses varies from person to person and from situation to situation. Also, God doesn't necessarily match the severity of the discipline to the gravity of our sin. He's not trying to get even with us. He's not out for vengeance. Rather, God measures the manner, level, and duration of the discipline in a way that will bring about the greatest good in us. After all, "God causes everything to work together for the good of those who love" Him (Romans 8:28). And *everything* includes His corrective discipline.

As all parents know, some children are soft hearted and sensitive to correction. Just a disapproving glare is enough to bring them back in line. Other children are strong willed and require repeated and sometimes severe consequences to train them up. The same is true with God's spiritual children. For some people, a few stern warnings are sufficient—such as reading the examples of disobedience and discipline in 1 Corinthians 10 or seeing the effects of somebody else's sin. For others, whose hearts have hardened against His warnings, God may send a severe and prolonged condition—such as the serpents in the wilderness or a protracted series of painful experiences. Yet in all cases, our heavenly Father's desired result is the same as it was thousands of years ago when the venomous snakes struck the rebellious children of Israel: repentance and restoration.

In short, God sends this discipline not because He hates us. Just the opposite! He exercises His discipline because He loves us. He can't bear to see His beloved children wander.

The book of Hebrews touches on this reality in chapter 12. We are ever caught in that constant tug-of-war between sin and righteousness, so God summons experiences, events, conditions, and people as instruments of His discipline.

The original readers of Hebrews had been experiencing a season of suffering that put their faith to the test. They were growing weary, tempted to give up (see Hebrews 12:3). No doubt, questions about God's goodness flooded their minds. Why were they suffering? Had God forsaken them?

The author of Hebrews provides some comforting correctives quoted from Proverbs 3:11-12—words with which the original

Jewish-Christian audience should have been familiar. But how easy it is to forget familiar truths amid pain and suffering! The author of Hebrews writes: "Have you forgotten the encouraging words God spoke to you as his children? He said, 'My child, don't make light of the LORD's discipline, and don't give up when he corrects you. For the LORD disciplines those he loves, and he punishes each one he accepts as his child'" (Hebrews 12:5-6).

In light of these wise words from Solomon, you and I need to see our struggles and trials as means God uses not only to challenge us but to change us. An informed faith will help you to meet each challenge and to experience real change. Remember: God's not harming you; He's healing you. He's not out to get you; He's out to grow you. You may never understand exactly how this particular pain or that specific struggle works to conform you to the image of His Son, but you can nevertheless trust that He knows you completely and can work even these things together for your ultimate good (see Romans 8:28).

Never forget Hebrews 12:7—"As you endure this divine discipline, remember that God is treating you as his own children." Four important principles arise from this fundamental truth.

God's Discipline Confirms That You Are, Indeed, His Child

Sometimes in the midst of your suffering, you may doubt that God truly loves you. But suffering actually proves His love: "Who ever heard of a child who is never disciplined by its father? If God doesn't discipline you as he does all of his children, it means that you are illegitimate and are not really his children at all" (Hebrews 12:7-8).

God's Discipline Deepens Your Spiritual Life

In Hebrews 12:9, the author employs an argument from the lesser to the greater. If we show respect for our earthly fathers when they discipline us, how much more should we submit to the discipline of our heavenly Father? The result of submitting to God is that you will truly experience the blessings of eternal life, which is to know God through Jesus Christ (John 17:3).

God's Discipline Is Always for Your Good

Because our earthly parents were just as fallen and imperfect as we are, they made mistakes. In most cases, though, they did "the best they knew how" (Hebrews 12:10). Yet your heavenly Father, who is perfect, never makes a mistake. Rather, "God's discipline is always good for us, so that we might share in his holiness" (verse 10).

God's Discipline, Though Painful, Is Profitable

Nobody likes to be reprimanded. Nobody likes to receive negative consequences for their actions. All discipline is painful in some way. Yet consistent, loving discipline will bring about positive change in your life. Hebrews 12:11 puts it this way: "Afterward there will be a peaceful harvest of right living for those who are trained in this way."

A faith informed by these four truths will allow you to meet God's loving discipline with hope.

OUR RESPONSE TO DISCIPLINE

Let's go back to Paul's description of the Israelites' experiences in the wilderness. Those events, Paul says, "were written down to warn us who live at the end of the age" (1 Corinthians 10:11). You and I are not immune to the same kinds of evil desires, idolatry, immorality, distrust, and complaining for which they were disciplined. If you think you've arrived at a place where you no longer need such warnings or where you're beyond the need for discipline, consider Paul's next words: "If you think you are standing strong, be careful not to fall" (verse 12).

It's a hard truth, but it must be told. Sometimes, God will not be pleased with our behavior or our attitude. It's important to do some soul-searching about this possibility. In fact, we should engage in personal reflection and response to God's warnings as often as we read our Bibles, pray, and practice other habits that nurture our intimacy with God.

To help you do this, let me share three practical suggestions for responding well to the warnings and to God's hand of discipline.

1. **Recognize and confess the true condition of your heart.** God wants to hear those same three words the Hebrew people uttered when they came face-to-face with their wickedness: "We have sinned" (Numbers 21:7). We need to confess our sin sooner rather than later. Don't play games with God. He doesn't toy around with our rebellion. The fact that you've "gotten away with it"—whatever "it" is—merely demonstrates the patience of our loving Father. Yet you can be sure that if you are truly a child of God, He's working on ways to steer you away from the ditch and back on the path. Wouldn't it be better to heed the warnings and to

recognize and confess the habits of your life *before* His hand of discipline falls?

2. **Deal with your inner attitudes.** The Hebrews were disciplined not only for their outward idolatry and immorality but also for their unbelief and ingratitude. We tend to get caught up with outward appearances— the obvious actions people can see. The actions that tend to bring immediate consequences in our relationships with others. But the Lord wants us to go deeper. Face your prideful, impatient, angry, negative, self-important, and critical mindsets. Those attitudes are the root of so many destructive words and actions. Dig them out of your life before they bring forth wicked fruit.

3. **Seek the inner healing you need from Christ.** Just as Moses lifted the serpent in the wilderness for physical healing (Numbers 21:8), God has lifted Christ on the Cross for you to look to for spiritual healing. You don't have to do penance, you don't have to pay alms, you don't have to win God's favor. Simply acknowledge your attitudes and actions, bring them before God, and look to Christ. He paid the price for your sin—*all* of your sin. Claim the forgiveness, reconciliation, and restoration He offers. And don't just glance at Him. Keep your eyes fixed on Him. See Christ and His work as an eternal rescue operation. Look to Him alone—and be healed.

In the training ground of life, God lovingly uses our afflictions to form us more and more into the likeness of His Son, as a father trains his children. When we heed the warnings and submit to Him, we will have a much different outlook on our struggles. We can face them with hope, knowing they are meant for our growth and healing.

CHAPTER 10

WHEN DOORS SLAM SHUT

God's Wisdom When You Meet Disappointment

WAY BACK IN 1959, I set foot on the campus of Dallas Theological Seminary as a first-year student. Cynthia and I had been married a little over four years. We had no children, so when we arrived, she was able to work to help put me through seminary. She found a job as an assistant to a CPA—a family man who loved spending time with his wife and their two small sons. They often entertained friends in their home.

As you can imagine, the man led a busy, fast-paced lifestyle. The nature of his successful accounting firm had him traveling quite a bit. But he did his best to keep all the balls in the air. On one occasion, though, he and his wife had invited guests over for dinner the very evening he was returning home on a flight from Florida to Dallas. Thankfully, his plane was almost ready for an on-time departure, and it looked like all was clicking along as planned. The flight was full, so he was relieved to know he had a seat reserved and would arrive home on time.

But those were the days before electronic ticketing, so having a paper ticket in hand didn't necessarily guarantee you a seat. Overbooking could be a problem. In rare instances, a person with a ticket and even a seat assignment could be bumped if somebody had purchased a ticket for the same seat just minutes before them.

That's what happened to our friend. In fact, he was already settled on the plane when the flight attendant informed him that he had to surrender his seat. Another passenger's ticket had higher priority. The hardest part was having to phone his wife and tell her he'd been bumped and wouldn't make it in time for their dinner.

What disappointment he felt as the ground crew closed the door, leaving him on the wrong side at the terminal. There he sat, waiting for the next flight to Dallas while his wife had to put the kids to bed, finish preparing the meal, and entertain their guests all on her own.

Later that evening, the original plane he had hoped to take from Florida to Texas crashed in the Gulf of Mexico. There were no survivors.

That closed door saved his life.

CLOSED DOORS ARE A GIFT FROM GOD

A lot of life's letdowns have a greater purpose in God's detailed orchestration of events designed to lead us, protect us, and provide for us.

That five-minute delay looking for your misplaced car key? Maybe the Lord kept you out of a deadly accident on your commute.

That part-time job you didn't get when you were in college? Maybe the Lord steered you away from a wrong career path.

That date who stood you up and made you feel so small all those years ago? Maybe it was God's way of keeping you available for the person He had in mind for you to meet and later marry.

The list could go on and on. You probably have your own stories of how a disappointment turned out to be a blessing in disguise. If X had happened, you would have missed out on Y. And if Y hadn't occurred, you would never have experienced Z. Life is full of these so-called God moments, when we realize He has been conducting every detail in ways we could never have imagined.

In fact, I've come to believe that rather than being great disappointments, closed doors can often be magnificent gifts from our sovereign God. Instead of resenting them, I've learned to accept them.

Our closed doors won't always be as dramatic as keeping us from boarding a doomed passenger plane. But that doesn't make them any less important in God's grand scheme. Also, you and I may never know the full reason for those lost opportunities. Yes, sometimes in hindsight we catch a glimpse of what might have been, and we are allowed to see God's wise providence shining through past setbacks.

Other times, though, all we know is God didn't want us to go in this or that direction. No explanation. No vindication. No aha! moment when we see how all the pieces fit together. In those cases, we can still trust in God's wisdom, goodness, and sovereignty—just as we can trust that the sun is still blazing behind the dark clouds when we can no longer see its brilliant light.

One thing's for sure. Our God is full of surprises. It's impossible for us to guess ahead of time what He's doing in our lives, where He's leading us, and what His ultimate plan includes. Our response to Him should be one of simple, childlike trust and obedience— acceptance without resistance.

That can be a difficult pill to swallow. Especially if we're the strong-willed type. After all, we have our plans too. And there's everything right about thinking through what we should do, where we should go, how we should accomplish our goals. God doesn't expect us simply to sit back, do nothing, and wait until we're absolutely certain we're taking a step in a divinely approved direction. The old cliché holds true—you can't steer a docked ship.

Yet sometimes in our desire to move forward, to keep busy, to complete our to-do list, we get fixated on our own direction, our own pace, our own pursuits. Add to this a strong will, and it can be painfully disappointing when God steps in, grabs us by the shoulder, and says, "Wrong way. I want you to go in *that* direction instead. Don't fight me!" Learning to plan tentatively and to hold our desires loosely can be tough.

WHEN GOD CLOSES DOORS

How hard it is to accept closed doors calmly and patiently! We live in a society in which no is rarely the final answer. We feel entitled to yes. If a student gets a bad grade on a test, he argues with the teacher. If a plaintiff loses a lawsuit, she appeals to a higher court. If an applicant doesn't make it into a particular university, he (or his parents) cry foul and push the issue into the public arena until the school changes its mind.

Not surprisingly, the Bible addresses the reality of obstacles in the lives of God's children. It provides helpful insights into why He may close some doors and open others. It also tells us what to do when we find ourselves with our nose against a door of opportunity that has just slammed shut in our face.

In Acts 16, we find the apostle Paul on his second missionary journey along with his companion, Silas. The two men are in need of God's guidance after several doors close for them. Clearly, the Lord's plans were different from what they expected.

Like us, Paul and Silas sometimes have to make last-minute adjustments when their goals don't work out. They can't explain the barriers. They couldn't have predicted them. They can't go around them. And they can't break through them. But they *do* have to accept them.

It's hard to view closed doors as gifts from God, but Paul and Silas have to learn how to make this shift in perspective mid-journey. They started out with their hearts set on taking the gospel message to those who had never heard it before—nothing thrills a missionary more than opening the light of the Good News to someone in spiritual darkness. Why wouldn't God open the door to every village, town, city, and country on every missionary's itinerary?

What makes Paul and Silas's experience of divine door-closing even more perplexing is that Paul had been on an earlier journey with Barnabas with no hint of hindrance. They met with wonderful success from one place to the next before returning to their home church in Antioch to give a glowing report (see Acts 13:4–14:26). As Paul plans his second journey, he proposes a perfectly reasonable and responsible plan: "Let's go back and visit each city where we previously preached the word of the Lord, to see how the new believers are doing" (Acts 15:36).

When Paul and Barnabas can't agree on whether to take John Mark along with them, they part ways (see Acts 15:36-39). With the church's blessing, Paul brings Silas along instead (15:40). Everything seems to be clicking. They travel easily through Syria and Cilicia, strengthening the infant churches (15:41). They even recruit a promising young man named Timothy in Lystra (16:1-4). He will prove to be not only a faithful companion and understudy but also Paul's protégé in pastoral ministry (see 1 and 2 Timothy). All the while, "the churches were strengthened in their faith and grew larger every day" (Acts 16:5).

Feeling the wind on their backs and anticipating success on the horizon, they must feel like clear skies and smooth sailing lie ahead.

Until they hit a few obstacles.

DIVINE PREVENTION

Having finished their return visits to churches planted in the first missionary journey, Paul, Silas, and Timothy intend to preach the word of God in the province of Asia to their west. However, "the Holy Spirit . . . prevented them" (Acts 16:6).

We aren't told *how* the Holy Spirit prevented them. Maybe Paul or Silas saw a vision. Maybe bad weather flooded the road. Maybe a fire blocked their path. We don't know. All we know is that the Holy Spirit was behind it. For some reason unknown to those eager missionaries, the door to Asia has slammed shut.

Ever anxious to advance the gospel into new regions, Paul and Silas shift into reverse, turn around, drop into low gear, and brace themselves for a different kind of off-road adventure. They travel northward through Phrygia and Galatia, perhaps intending to re-enter the region of Asia from the north. They come to the borders of Mysia, north of Asia, and prepare to go northeast to Bithynia, the region of the modern city of Istanbul, the connection between Asia Minor and Europe. Yet, "again the Spirit of Jesus did not allow them to go there" (Acts 16:7).

Interestingly, the word used in verse 7 for preventing or disallowing the apostles to advance may be derived from a nautical term for leaving an anchor in the sea.[1] Instead of the smooth sailing they had experienced after their launch from Antioch, it now feels like they are paddling against a dragging anchor.

This time, the text says the door to Bithynia was closed by "the Spirit of Jesus" (16:7). We get no details, just the impression that resistance would have been as futile as rowing against high waves and a hurricane wind. Though it must have been hard for Paul to understand, we read nothing about him arguing with God or attempting to force his way into Asia. There is acceptance without resistance.

We've all been in Paul's place—doors blocked left and right. It's tempting to push on those doors, try to pick their locks, or maybe look for a side entrance or open window to crawl through. Or perhaps we just keep pounding on the door, shouting our complaints, reasoning with God, bargaining with Him: "Lord, could you please open this door?" *Knock, knock, knock.* "Come on, Lord, after all the years I've served You, can't I have this one thing?" *Thump, thump, thump.* "Think of all the good I could do if You would just open this door and let me through!" *Bang, bang, bang.* "Okay, Lord, this isn't funny anymore. You know I've been preparing for this opportunity all my life. *Let me in!*"

Paul doesn't take the bargaining approach. Nor does he throw his hands up and go home in discouragement. Instead, he keeps moving ahead.

The doors God closed to Bithynia and Asia really mean they can go in only one direction: west through Mysia toward the port city of Troas (Acts 16:8), at the edge of the Aegean Sea.

Finally it becomes clear why God kept them away from those other seemingly perfect ministry opportunities.

He had something much, much bigger in mind.

GOD OPENS A DOOR

When they come to Troas, Paul, Silas, and Timothy stand at the shores of the Aegean Sea—the end of the road, so to speak. From there the only easy route is back east or south into Asia—the very region blocked by the Holy Spirit earlier.

In the biblical text, a period stands at the end of the word "Troas" (Acts 16:8). Our tendency is to move quickly beyond that punctuation, but in that little space between verses 8 and 9, we can imagine a host of emotions—frustration, puzzlement, impatience, confusion, maybe even doubt. Perhaps mixed with these feelings are excitement, faith, confidence, and a sense of adventure.

I would love to have been a bug on the wall, eavesdropping on the conversation as Paul, Silas, and Timothy tried to make sense of what God was doing. I might have heard questions like "What now?" and "What on earth is God doing?" and "Why in the world are we in Troas?" I like to think that after tossing around ideas and offering up some desperate prayers, they agree to get a good night's sleep and to talk over their options in the morning.

After they retire that evening under the vast array of stars in the heavens, with the waters of the Aegean splashing along the shoreline, God shows up. "That night," we read, "Paul had a vision: A man from Macedonia in northern Greece was standing there, pleading with him, 'Come over to Macedonia and help us!'" (Acts 16:9).

Let me pause here to make a point. God doesn't always show up like this with a clear path forward. Often, He keeps us in a holding pattern for weeks, months—even years. But in this case, after several weeks of closed doors and uncertainty, God sends a reassuring vision to the men through Paul. Remember, too, that Paul was an apostle and Silas was a prophet (Acts 15:32). They were unique instruments of divine revelation, and even they had to experience some closed doors before they discovered their answer.

You and I are living after the age of apostles and prophets. It's not likely we will see a vision that tells us where to turn. We should expect to hunker down and trust God to work through closed and opened doors and in ways that may not match our own plans or expected timetables. And we may never get a clear explanation for why God wanted us to move in direction B instead of direction A. So it is in the life of faith. Never forget that!

In Paul's case, as the apostles and prophets were still laying the foundation of the church, the Spirit worked in ways that aren't what we would call normative today. God does work in strange, un-expected, and mysterious ways. And He may use surprising methods to get our attention and to steer our course. But we should not camp out at every crossroads of life waiting for a vision or dream. Instead, we need to keep moving. God will open and close doors by His sovereign hand.

PIVOTAL OPPORTUNITIES

The message in Paul's vision seems urgent: "Come help us!" It has become clear that God's plan was for them to depart from Asia Minor and break new ground in Europe—certainly, much farther out than they had originally planned. God's vision for Paul's ministry is even bigger than the apostle's plans! I love the men's immediate response: "So we decided to leave for Macedonia at once" (Acts 16:10).

Please pause and notice one other detail in this passage. It may not seem like much at first, but if you think about it, it's big. Starting with their departure to Macedonia, when referring to the apostolic ministry team, the narrative shifts from third-person plural "they" (verse 8) to the first-person plural "we" (verse 10)—"we decided to leave." Did you catch that?

Acts 16:10 is the first of five "we" references in the book of Acts (see Acts 16:10-17; 20:5-15; 21:1-18; 27:1-37; 28:1-16). These shifts to the first-person plural mark places in the narrative when the author, Luke, personally joins the ministry team. From that point on, Luke is an eyewitness to the events, until Paul and Silas depart on their own again (Acts 16:40).

Think about how God coordinated the timing of events in such a way that Paul, Silas, and Timothy would end up in Troas just as Luke, too, is in that city. Their "chance" meeting loops Luke into Paul's wider ministry circle and sets him on course to write the Gospel of Luke and the book of Acts. Also, as a physician, he may have connections in Troas. God's providential addition of Luke to the team makes it easier to transition to a new mission field, new culture, new language, new customs.

Because he knows his way around, Dr. Luke can make it possible for the missionary team to catch a ship to Macedonia right away (Acts 16:11). I can imagine that physician hearing of their plans to cross into Macedonia and responding with "Hey, I can get you there. In fact, there's a ship leaving today. I know the captain. I've been to Neapolis and Philippi several times. I'll show you around!"

Not only does God open a door of new ministry opportunities, He also sovereignly provides the means to get there and minister effectively.

What a pivotal moment in the spread of the gospel "to the ends of the earth"! Everything comes together perfectly. And to think the opportunity would have been missed had Paul, Silas, and Timothy doubled down on their insistence to enter Asia or Bithynia, to pound on those closed doors until their knuckles bled and the doors fell off their hinges!

But they don't. Already around AD 49, they understand an important truth about their Lord Jesus Christ that wouldn't be clearly stated in the book of Revelation for about another fifty years: "What he opens, no one can close; and what he closes, no one can open" (3:7). More on that in a few moments.

Suddenly, the mystery of the closed doors is solved. In Troas, their weeks of head-scratching and brow-furrowing change to wide-eyed excitement. I like to picture those men laughing together on that ship crossing the northern edge of the Aegean Sea, bound for Macedonia. Smiles stretch across their faces as they connect the dots, realizing what they would have missed if they had gotten their way.

The words of Isaiah 55:8-9 come to life for that band of disciples as they ponder the path on which God has led them: "'My thoughts are nothing like your thoughts,' says the LORD. 'And my ways are far beyond anything you could imagine. For just as the heavens are higher than the earth, so my ways are higher than your ways and my thoughts higher than your thoughts.'"

How excited they are, standing on the deck of that ship!

THE DOOR NO ONE CAN SHUT

Back to the book of Revelation. Christ describes Himself in his letter to the church in Philadelphia as the one with the authority to open and close doors: "This is the message from the one who is holy and true, the one who has the key of David. What he opens, no one can close; and what he closes, no one can open" (3:7).

This self-description draws on language from Isaiah 22. During the reign of King Hezekiah, the royal treasurer, Eliakim, had complete authority to keep watch over the king's riches. With that responsibility came a key that could open the vault. Isaiah 22:22 indicates the expansive power entrusted to Eliakim: "I will give him the key to the house of David—the highest position in the royal court. When he opens doors, no one will be able to close them; when he closes doors, no one will be able to open them."

In the message to the Philadelphians, Jesus describes Himself as the One who holds that authority in the most exalted sense. As the Davidic King, the long-awaited Messiah, Jesus alone is heir to the "key to the house of David." As such, He can impart blessing or withhold it, grant power or deny it, open doors or close them. He has complete sovereignty over the church, over the world, and over all creation.

The church in Philadelphia needs to hear this reassuring word from the One who exercises absolute sovereign control over all circumstances. That small church has difficulty coping with their smallness. Jesus tells them, "You have little strength, yet you obeyed my word and did not deny me" (Revelation 3:8). Even though they lack some of the size, resources, and influence that larger, more significant churches enjoyed, Christ points out that they have tremendous opportunities. He encourages them with these words: "I have opened a door for you that no one can close" (verse 8).

I've seen all sorts of explanations in commentaries on what Jesus' statement means. Does it refer to an open door to heaven, reminding them of their eternal home?[2] Or does it refer to an open door for ministry, an overlooked opportunity to influence their city or region for the gospel?[3] In cases like this, it's best to set speculation aside and let the New Testament interpret itself. Consider the following verses:

> Upon arriving in Antioch, they called the church together and reported everything God had done through them and how he had opened the door of faith to the Gentiles, too.
>
> ACTS 14:27

> There is a wide-open door for a great work here, although many oppose me.
>
> I CORINTHIANS 16:9

When I came to the city of Troas to preach the Good News
of Christ, the Lord opened a door of opportunity for me.

2 CORINTHIANS 2:12

In light of these passages, it seems most likely Christ is reminding
the Philadelphian church that despite their smallness, He has huge
opportunities for them. Though they may feel as if doors to effective
ministry have been closed because of their circumstances, Christ has
actually opened a door wide. All they need is to step through.

As the geographic gateway to the East, the city of Philadelphia
was situated at an important crossroads in Asia. People with a variety
of languages and cultures would have come through all the time.
That dynamic may not have contributed to a large, stable congregation, but it certainly provided plenty of opportunities for proclaim-
ing the gospel far and wide simply by being faithful where they were
planted.

Maybe you have felt like that little church in Philadelphia. Maybe
right now you find yourself in circumstances where your potential for
ministry is hampered by limitations beyond your control. It could
be that the environment at your place of employment stifles any
spiritual conversations. Or perhaps your neighbors are as secular or
even anti-Christian as you've ever seen. Perhaps your stage of life has
you stuck at home with small children most of the day—or living in
isolation because of an illness or disability.

Your situation may feel like a long hallway of closed, locked doors,
preventing you from thriving in ministry.

But don't look at it that way. Remember the One who holds the
key—who can open and shut as He wills. While your circumstances

may feel limiting, look again. What open doors might you be over-looking right in front of your nose? God may be using the closed doors to accomplish certain results in your life—or to equip you for something much larger. They may be turning your attention away from yourself and back to God. Maybe He's teaching you to trust Him completely, to wait on Him patiently, and to surrender to Him and His timing entirely.

INSURMOUNTABLE OPPORTUNITIES

I'm convinced that you and I spend too much of our lives staring at closed doors. We're dejected, disappointed, maybe even offended that God wouldn't let us through. We make our plans, plot our courses, and push off with enthusiasm—only to be waylaid by some insurmountable obstacle that sends us back to square one.

All these closed doors make me think about the words of cartoon-ist Walt Kelly in his old *Pogo* comic strip: "We are confronted with insurmountable opportunities." What a great, paradoxical turn of phrase: *insurmountable opportunities*! The truth is, God closes doors to the logical, easy path in order to open routes to opportunities that we have viewed as insurmountable.

I think about the Israelites fleeing Egypt and heading for the Promised Land, the Egyptian army behind them to the west, a long shoreline of the Red Sea stretching north and south. They stood at the edge of that massive sea, about to be overcome by the enemy. What an insurmountable opportunity for God to step in and do the impossible! You know how the story turned out. Take courage from it and trust God to guide your own steps.

I want to wrap up our discussion about what to do when doors slam shut by considering four principles you can use whenever you face obstacles or disappointments.

1. **Because God is sovereign, He's in full control of all the doors in your life.** I find great comfort in knowing God is God and I am not. The longer I've lived, the less put off I am when God slams doors shut and moves me in another direction. Yes, early on in life and ministry it irritated me. I'd sometimes pout, maybe even grumble. But I finally discovered He always opens new doors of opportunity I could never have imagined. I'm not at all offended when a good, all-wise, sovereign God steers me in a better direction. In fact, I'm grateful. And you should be too.

2. **God takes full responsibility for the doors He closes to you and those He opens.** It's not your responsibility. It's His. So, stop pounding on those closed doors and trying to pry them open. Leave them with God. He can—and will—deal with what's behind them in His own way. You don't need to worry about them. The door God closes to you may be opened for somebody else. That's His business. Move along, knowing that the Lord will guide you where He needs you.

3. **When a door closes to something good, it will often lead you to an open door of something better.** When God closes a door, it doesn't necessarily mean that your plan was bad. It doesn't always mean that He's keeping you from evil or from danger. It may very well be that He's steering you away from something that would have been good. But where He leads you instead is much better. Remember the meandering

route taken by Paul, Silas, and Timothy? Ministry in Asia and Bithynia would have been good, no doubt. But passing through the gateway to continental Europe pushed the church farther out much faster than anybody could have expected. We know other missionaries and apostles covered the areas of Asia and Bithynia. It's not that God didn't want the gospel to go there. It's that God had bigger, better plans for Paul at the time. So, when God closes the door on something you know would be good, brace yourself. He may have something even better in mind.

4. **Not until you walk through the door God opens will you realize the necessity for closing the others.** Paul couldn't have imagined exactly what he was walking into when he set foot in Troas. But as soon as he boarded that ship for Macedonia and put the pieces together, he undoubtedly recognized God's fingerprints all over their adventure. Perfect timing. Perfect planning. Even if he had strategized for months, Paul couldn't have worked out that itinerary of divine appointments and history-changing opportunities. Looking back, what seemed like a meandering path turned out to be a logical, dot-to-dot route to God's perfect will. Someday you may be able to look back on your own life and trace a similar pattern of His design.

So, when doors slam shut in your path, don't be discouraged. Instead, like Paul and Silas, wait expectantly for a better opportunity. When it comes, step through the door God opens for you, and accept it with gratitude.

CHAPTER 11

WHEN SOLITUDE DRIVES US DEEPER

God's Wisdom When You Feel Alone

I HAD BEEN MARRIED ONLY TWO AND a half years when the US Marine Corps sent me overseas to the distant island known as "the Rock"—Okinawa. I'm not ashamed to admit I was totally unprepared for it. There I was, on a massive troopship headed for the other side of the world, eight thousand miles away from my wife, my family, and all my friends—living with people I didn't know. I fully expected to wither away in loneliness, self-pity, and depression. Little did I realize, God had other purposes in mind.

Sometimes we get so caught up in our misery that we forget to stop, step back, and ask, "What does God want to teach me through this?" How easy it is to lose sight of the lessons God has for us in every situation. In one time of isolation, I came across an insightful statement from Malcolm Muggeridge worth repeating: "Every happening, great and small, . . . is a parable whereby God speaks to us; and the art of life is to get the message."[1]

I can't help but wonder if most of us completely miss the message God has for us in our circumstances. It's easy to overlook in the seemingly disjointed, random, unexpected happenings in our lives—forgetting that God does, indeed, work all these things together for our good (see Romans 8:28).

In previous chapters, we delved into some deep subjects: when troubles come and stay and when suffering makes its mark on our lives, when heartbreaks and calamities crash in and when giants and thorns afflict us. We've seen examples of patient endurance amid trials as well as pictures of faith in response to loving discipline and closed doors.

In this chapter and the next one, I want to focus more intentionally on the inner attitudes of the heart in response to these inevitable "whens" of life. In the final chapter, we'll also look at how God makes us more like Christ through humility. But first, let's explore how to turn often unexpected and unwelcome isolation and loneliness into a positive, life-giving discipline of solitude.

ALONENESS, NOT LONELINESS

The message God had for me through my experience on Okinawa left a permanent impression on my character. If the Lord had put that message into words, it would have been something like this: "I want to remove from you every crutch, everything you are familiar with, so I can have your full attention, because My plan is to change the entire direction of your life."

Achieving that goal required driving me into solitude so He could get my undivided attention.

Now, I confess I missed His message for a number of months as I wallowed in my loneliness. But in the same way that the words of a street sign veiled in a fog begin to clear up as you draw nearer, little by little God's message began to materialize. I had been viewing that stint on Okinawa as a rather rude disruption of my happy life. Yet I came to accept it as an essential part of God's forming and fashioning me, preparing me for a ministry journey involving spells of spiritual desperation that would drive me to my knees. I wouldn't have been able to see that message clearly through the mists of self-absorption had it not been for those seventeen months, totally removed from all things familiar. Solitude has a way of driving us deeper.

And I know I'm not alone in this. Many people I know express angst over forced separation from loved ones. It takes a mental, emotional, and spiritual toll on us. Maybe you yourself have experienced a feeling of utter lostness, like a vessel adrift, a growing sense of displacement and remoteness from the safe shores of stable relationships. In unguarded moments, even if you're a mature believer, you may entertain an alien thought you've never pondered before: *Where is God? If He's everywhere present, and Jesus promises never to leave us, why do I feel so alone?* It may seem like the ever-reliable light in your lighthouse has been extinguished. The world turns dark.

In seasons of loneliness, instead of letting the raging ocean of despair pull our thoughts and emotions into its deep void, we can turn our attention to the light of truth God is shining into that darkness. Instead of viewing these times as forced loneliness, we can see them as divinely prescribed solitude. Instead of demanding explanations and relief from God, we can diligently seek out the truths He wants to teach us.

Times of solitude are really opportunities for in-depth self-examination. The change of pace, the silence, the solace—these provide an ideal context for cultivating greater awareness of where we really are spiritually—and where God wants us to be. Times of solitude afford an occasion to push pause on our high-speed existence. To look within. To ask, "Lord, is there anything in my life that needs special attention?"

In the realm of spiritual disciplines, "solitude" doesn't refer to personal privacy. It's not a two-second breather or a ten-minute coffee break away from others. It's not getting away from the big-city-paced bustle and retreating to a metaphorical dry desert of inactivity. If we plop down on a sand dune of seclusion with no strategy for nourishment, we'll wither in loneliness and return to our lives parched rather than refreshed.

No, solitude for spiritual refreshment and reflection is more like arriving at an oasis—an intimate paradise where we can see our own reflection in the glassy pools of clear water, feed on the luscious fruit of God's Word, and fellowship with the Lord as Adam and Eve once walked with Him in that magnificent garden. In our oasis of solitude, much of the intrusive clutter of life is left behind in the desert.

AN INVITATION TO INSPECTION

In our spiritual oasis of solitude, God opens our eyes to blights on our character that require confession and cleansing. Afterward, when the Spirit of God has restored our soul, we can experience victory over our deepest struggles in the journey toward Christlikeness.

David invited the Lord to do this kind of work in his own life in the closing verses of Psalm 139:

> Search me, O God, and know my heart;
>> test me and know my anxious thoughts.
> Point out anything in me that offends you,
>> and lead me along the path of everlasting
>> life.

PSALM 139:23-24

What an appropriate prayer for going deep when we're steeped in solitude. When we've been granted freedom from the rat race, it's the perfect time to ask the Lord to probe us, to inspect the inner turmoil of our hearts, to reveal to us those attitudes and actions that need to be fully explored and openly confessed so we can enter into an abundant life (see John 10:10).

As we're speeding down the fast lane of our everyday world, we're so wrapped up in responsibilities, obligations, assignments, demands, and deadlines that we rarely pause and take time to look deep within. That's what David's praying for: "Search me, O God."

Of course, God already knew what was in David's heart. He knows what is in our hearts too. He knows all about us. In fact, the psalm begins, "O LORD, you have examined my heart and know everything about me. You know when I sit down or stand up. You know my thoughts even when I'm far away" (Psalm 139:1-2). Wherever we go, whatever we do, the Lord is already there (see 139:3-12). He's aware of every move we make, every thought we have, every word we speak. In fact, He knows us better than we know ourselves. As

David says, "Such knowledge is too wonderful for me, too great for me to understand!" (139:6).

Yet the Lord wants to reach deep into your innermost being, to bring to the surface of your awareness anything that causes disquiet, anxiety, anger, and sin, and to give you the opportunity to deal with each painful reality. We all have those contaminants in our hearts that poison our thoughts, taint our words, and twist our actions.

But to deal with these inner toxins, you need alone time. Not "me time." Not "free time." And definitely not a time for sulking in self-pity. How valuable are those protracted times spent in reflective, meditative, and restorative *solitude*!

When we refuse to set aside those times ourselves, our sovereign God will see to it that we get them. He will bring occasions into our lives that force us to be still and know that He is God (see Psalm 46:10)—*and we are not*!

THE DISCIPLINE OF REFLECTION

As uncomfortable as it may be to hear, God will sometimes orchestrate your circumstances for the sole purpose of stopping you in your tracks. It could be as simple as a missed flight that forces you to sit and think for a number of hours. It could be bad weather that leaves you stranded. It could be downed power lines or car trouble. It could be an injury, an illness, a lengthy time of recovery from surgery, or even the loss of a loved one. These and other happenings can push you into unexpected, even unwelcome isolation.

What does God want from you during those periods when your life has slowed down or come to a sudden halt? He wants you to do what you're always supposed to do: He wants you to make the most of the time you have (see Ephesians 5:16). He wants you to grow deeper in every way as He shapes you to become more and more like Christ (Ephesians 4:15). He wants you to allow the Spirit to fashion in you godly traits of Christlike character (Ephesians 4:23).

But godliness doesn't happen automatically or easily. It comes as the result of discipline. In chapter 9, we discussed the idea of *corrective* discipline as it related to the Israelites wandering in the wilderness. Now, let's take a few minutes to examine the concept of *constructive* discipline a little more closely.

In a very personal letter of exhortation and encouragement, Paul writes his mentee, Timothy, urging him not to waste his time on a host of distractions that would only frustrate his pursuit of Christlikeness. "Instead," he says, "train yourself to be godly" (1 Timothy 4:7). The NASB renders the same command as "discipline yourself for the purpose of godliness."

Did you notice that's a command? Paul doesn't merely suggest, "Sit back and wait for God to miraculously zap you into godliness." Godliness doesn't just emerge in our lives. It doesn't seep into our souls like spiritual osmosis. If you meet people with a calm, consistent, godly character, you can be sure they endured a long and arduous process of discipline in days past to achieve it. They weren't born that way. They didn't go to sleep one day as immature, self-centered sinners and lift their heads from the pillow in the morning as mature, others-centered saints. It takes discipline to get there.

In fact, the word translated "train" or "discipline" is the Greek word *gymnazō*. We derive our English word "gymnasium" from it. In his book on disciplines of the Christian life, R. Kent Hughes says this about *gymnazō*: "By New Testament times, it referred to exercise and training in general. But even then it was, as it remains, a word with the smell of the gym in it—the sweat of a good workout."[2]

Continuing his gymnasium imagery, Paul says, "Physical training is good, but training for godliness is much better, promising benefits in this life and in the life to come" (1 Timothy 4:8). In a classic argument from the lesser to the greater—from the physical to the spiritual—he also underscores an important point: this is not a lazy person's task. He continues, "This is why we work hard and continue to struggle, for our hope is in the living God" (4:10). Hard work. Struggle. It's as if Paul is Timothy's personal spiritual trainer, establishing his workout routine, spotting him as he does heavy spiritual lifting, encouraging him as he strengthens his spiritual muscles.

The same holds true for us today. All our study Bibles, Christian music, challenging devotionals, and online resources haven't excused us from heavy lifting. They've given us an array of workout equipment, but we still need to go through the tough conditioning and the struggle toward spiritual maturity. If bodybuilding is our goal, we need to work hard at it. If preparing for a marathon is our goal, we need to train for it. And if godliness is our goal, we must take the steps necessary to attain it.

But what are those steps? Look at the advice Paul gave to Timothy.

Focus on Reading the Scriptures

Paul first tells his young protégé, "Focus on reading the Scriptures to the church, encouraging the believers, and teaching them" (1 Timothy 4:13). In the first century most people didn't have their own copy of the Scriptures. Written works were expensive, copying Scripture by hand required the skill of a professional, and many people were illiterate. So, most believers had to gather to hear Scripture read to them. That's why Timothy was exhorted to read Scripture aloud to the gathered people of God. Today, whether we read it in our own Bibles or hear it as an audio recording, we need God's Word to inspire and instruct us.

Keep a Close Watch on How You Live

In verse 16, Paul says, "Keep a close watch on how you live and on your teaching. Stay true to what is right." Now, it's been decades since our house was childproof. You know—when you set fragile things on higher shelves, cover electrical outlets, barricade stairs, and make sure anything small enough to fit in a child's mouth is out of reach. Today, if young children were to visit us, our home would be a gauntlet of dangers for them. I'd have to keep a close eye on their every move. I'm pretty sure every table corner would be a hazard, every surface a risk.

With the same kind of hawkeyed focus we'd give to keeping a curious toddler safe in our homes, we need to "keep a close watch" on the things we believe, the doctrines we accept, the moral principles we embrace. In case you haven't noticed, our modern world is no safer for children of God than my home is for an unguarded two-year-old.

The kind of consistent, persevering discipline Paul has in mind doesn't come easily. Or naturally. And it doesn't come when our schedules are so full that our electronic calendars look like cityscapes or traffic jams. This is why God has to clear away the clutter. It's not a punishment, but a blessing. Not a scourge of loneliness, but an opportunity for time alone with God.

THE EXAMPLE OF JESUS

If we're to walk as Jesus walked, live as Jesus lived, and conduct ourselves in ways that conform us to His image, solitude will be a vital part of our discipline. When we read the Gospel of Mark, we see that Jesus keeps a fast-paced schedule. In fact, Mark regularly uses the word "immediately" to transition between scenes. It's as if Jesus finishes a sermon, completes a task, answers a challenge—then immediately moves on to the next responsibility. We get the picture that Jesus' days are packed with activities, people, and pressures that could easily have led a normal person to a stress-induced mental burnout or physical breakdown.

Yet Mark also notes that Jesus takes time to step away from the busyness: "Before daybreak the next morning, Jesus got up and went out to an isolated place to pray" (Mark 1:35). See that word *isolated*? That's solitude. Even Jesus—the God-Man—knows enough to withdraw from the flurry of activities to recharge, refocus, and refresh. Jesus picks a time and place that will afford Him the most privacy. He never plans on staying there all day. After all, He has a lot of work to do. But He knows the value of silence and being alone with His Father.

The next line tells us that Simon and the rest of the disciples hunt Him down, and when they find Him, they say, "Everyone is looking for you" (1:37). Apparently, the immediate circle of disciples and other followers don't appreciate Jesus' need for quiet time as much as He does. All they see is the public work that needs to be done; they don't understand the private needs of the Worker.

But Jesus knows. He needs that time away from all the demands so He will have the physical, mental, emotional, and spiritual energy to do the work. Remember, Jesus is fully God, but He also took upon Himself full humanity, with the same needs for food and rest that you and I have. And as the God-Man, He knows the limits of His physical body even better than we know ours.

It is essential that we take His example seriously. Just as solitude was necessary for Jesus, it's equally necessary for us. Yes, it's easy to think of solitude as equivalent to burning money or sitting on your hands. The world keeps rushing by, and if you sit out of the race, you're sure you'll fall behind. You may feel the need to have people around you all the time. Or maybe you like to have a constant flow of information pouring in—reading, watching, listening, attending one meeting after another to keep from falling behind.

Candidly, I don't recall ever learning anything profound in a crowd or in a cacophony. Don't get me wrong—I love people. (And I've been told I can be a loud conversationalist.) But in silence and solitude, I'm best able to sift the essentials from the nonessentials of life. I can sort through the good, the better, and the best. That can't be done in the company of people and environments so noisy you can't even think.

May I ask? Can you remember the last time you were alone in quietness? I'm not talking about a car ride with the radio blasting or a program playing through your headphones. When did you last deliberately set aside time for genuine solitude? If you're like most modern men and women, you're having a hard time answering that question. You're continually dealing with intentional or unexpected distractions.

We owe it to ourselves, to God, and to those around us to

withdraw, as Jesus did, and find solace in silence. We need to overcome the knee-jerk reaction against it. We have to banish all those excuses for why we don't need it, or why it just isn't for us.

Sometimes it's the pride of self-sufficiency that keeps us from solitude. Sometimes it's fear. Maybe you are afraid of being alone. I get that. You may not yet have experienced the difference between "loneliness" and "aloneness." Or perhaps you shake your head and wonder, "What in the world would I do in all that silence and solitude?" To begin with, you pray. You sit and think in silence. You meditate on selected Scriptures. You consider the thoughts and struggles of your heart. You reflect on your responses and attitudes. And you let the Lord probe your soul.

ALONE TIME IN ARABIA

When Paul instructed Timothy concerning personal discipline, he wrote as a man who knew the value of solitude for developing intimacy with God. In the autobiographical portions of Galatians 1, Paul provides personal insight into the first steps of his spiritual journey as a disciple of the Lord Jesus Christ.

In his life before meeting his Savior, Paul had been a zealous adherent of Judaism, as we saw in chapter 8. So zealous, in fact, that when he first hears of the followers of Jesus, he persecutes the church and tries to destroy it (see Galatians 1:13). In his own words: "I was far ahead of my fellow Jews in my zeal for the traditions of my ancestors" (1:14).

Paul's name was feared among Christians in those early years. He was like a religious terrorist, hell-bent on wiping the church off the face of the earth. It seems he would have continued in his acts of religious terrorism if God hadn't had other plans. In a dramatic and sudden twist, the Lord Jesus steps in, reveals Himself to Paul, and calls him to "proclaim the Good News about Jesus to the Gentiles" (1:16). We can read about his Damascus road life transformation in Acts 9. That encounter with Jesus not only changes Paul's story, but it also changes history.

After that miraculous conversion to Christ, Paul steps into the next phase of his life. Remember, he already had years of training in Jewish law and customs in the prestigious school of Gamaliel (see Acts 22:3). Yet all that training needs to be undone. The rabbinical traditions had tied a thick theological knot in Paul's mind, and it would take time to work it loose.

What is God's plan for the kind of discipline needed to retrain Paul for his new God-given mission as an apostle to the Gentiles?

Solitude.

Paul writes, "I did not rush out to consult with any human being. Nor did I go up to Jerusalem to consult with those who were apostles before I was. Instead, I went away into Arabia" (Galatians 1:16-17).

I want you to study those last five words: "I went away into Arabia." Paul leaves a lot of questions unanswered. Why did he go? What did he do there? How long did he stay? Though people have speculated about these questions for centuries, Paul doesn't answer them, so we don't know the details.

Arabia is a big place—the vast desert region east and southeast of Damascus. Paul doesn't pinpoint the place, but one thing is clear—it is far away from Jerusalem and Damascus, where the apostles and teachers of the Christian faith are centered. Instead of enrolling in Jerusalem Bible College or Damascus Theological Seminary, Paul deliberately withdraws from the crowds and spends an extended period all alone with the Messiah. Reflecting on his experience on the road to Damascus. Coming to terms with his newfound faith. And thinking through the implications for the mission to the Gentiles.

The insightful British pastor and author F. B. Meyer puts it this way:

> He wanted to be alone, to reflect on all that he had seen;
> to coordinate, if possible, the new with the old, the
> present with the past. For this he must have uninterrupted
> leisure, and he hungered for the isolation and solitude
> of the wilderness . . . but, above all things, he wanted to
> be alone with Jesus, to know Him and the power of his
> resurrection.[3]

What happened to Paul in Arabia? A complete alteration of his inner person. His allegiances are flipped. His priorities are rearranged. His zeal for God is filled with knowledge. He had been a violent aggressor, engaged in the bounty hunting of believers. Now, for being a believer himself, he will spend the rest of his life as a target of others' violence. Talk about an "extreme makeover"!

In Paul's Arabia, I imagine the howling winds sweeping around him, blowing up sand in his already sun-scorched face. Despite the discomfort and isolation, Paul is exactly where the Lord wants him. Meyer continues,

> Month after month he wandered to and fro, now sharing the
> rough fare of some Essene community, or the lot of a family

of Bedouins; now swept upwards in heavenly fellowship, and again plunged into profound meditation. . . .

But deeper than all was God's work with his soul. Grain by grain his proud self-reliance and impetuosity were worn away.[4]

OUR ARABIA

What does Paul's time in Arabia have to do with us? Frankly, everything.

When Paul is alone in Arabia, he isn't *lonely* in Arabia. In those long days away from all distractions, Paul goes deep with God. The Spirit of the Lord impresses upon his mind the truths of his new-found faith. The One he had blasphemed as a false messiah he now embraces as his very own Lord and Savior. No doubt he comes to grips with how Jesus fulfilled the Old Testament prophecies, wrestles with the reality of His atoning death and miraculous resurrection, and plumbs the depths of the doctrine of justification by grace alone through faith alone in Christ alone. We can only imagine the profound mysteries he explores in those hours of solitude with the Lord.

How about us? What should you and I do in our times of forced aloneness—when circumstances beyond our control waylay us for a season? Should you sit around feeling lonely and sad? Fret over those hours or days as time wasted? Obsess about the people you can't see or the things you can't get done? It's tempting to slip into those lines of thought. But you don't have to.

Instead, you can redeem those seasons of solitude as divinely appointed opportunities to go deeper with God. Remember that God stops us in our tracks for a reason. He will send you to your own

Arabia to teach you vital truths you need to hear from Him—truths too often drowned out by the busyness and the noisiness of daily life.

So, my charge to you in light of Paul's experience is to make the most of your personal periods of solitude. In fact, carve out space in that jam-packed schedule for some time alone with God. There's no reason to wait for God to force it on you. I've discovered that if we make solitude a regular discipline of our walk with Christ, when those periods of isolation are brought about by circumstances under God's control, it will be much easier to accept them and, in fact, embrace them. We'll be practiced at it.

But you see, the way we're put together, we buck at the constraints. We resent the unexpected. After all, we have people to see, places to go, things to do! We get irritated over the fact that we can't get back to our normal routines. We can't check the boxes on our to-do list. We can't meet our precious deadlines.

But that's the whole point!

God doesn't scream His message. He waits for us to get it. Remember the words of Malcolm Muggeridge: "The art of life is to get the message." Are you getting it? Do you long to have a closer walk with Jesus Christ? Are you willing to pray the prayer of David from a place of solitude? "Search me, O God, and know my heart." When we're stuck in our own Arabia, such prayers come easily. And in that holy silence, it's so much easier to hear our Lord's response.

You know what happens in your Arabia? When you add solitude to your regimen of constructive discipline? You're no longer pulled by the allure of the limelight, the appeal of public adulation, the yearning for self-centered living, the hunger for applause. Paul lived for those distractions before his Arabia. Afterwards, he ran from them.

My desire for you is that you make the most of those times of solitude. Rather than grinding your teeth in irritation, see them as a gift. Usually unexpected, often involuntary, they're thrust upon us like sudden thunderstorms on a summer afternoon. Yet it is through those seasons that God speaks to us most clearly. When I finally began to see the benefits of my months away from all the comforts and crutches of home and accepted God's hand in leading me to Okinawa, my life began to be transformed. It was then and there I realized He was calling me to serve Him in the ministry. It took solitude to awaken that realization within me.

Only God knows the plans He has for *you*. Set aside those times to be alone with Him. Listen to His voice. He is saying, as it were, "Here I am. I long to meet with you, to take you on a journey deeper into your own life. You'll see yourself as you really are—and I'll show you what you can become. You'll delve into deep truths and explore new heights of unimaginable glory. All you need to do is embrace the solitude, take My hand, and let Me lead you."

CHAPTER 12

WHEN ADVERSITY LEADS TO HUMILITY

God's Wisdom When Struggles Make You More Like Christ

In 1974, I had the privilege of meeting Francis Schaeffer. You may remember that name. If you don't, it's not too late to catch up on some of his classics: *The God Who Is There*, *True Spirituality*, and *How Should We Then Live?* Back in his day, he took the Christian world by storm. His analysis of Christian culture, history, and contemporary issues was as relevant then as it was prophetic for our times.

It was from Schaeffer that I first heard ten words that have informed my approach to ministry for almost fifty years: "We must do the Lord's work in the Lord's way."[1]

Those words are embedded in my mind. Their truth and relevance for life and ministry are both ancient and enduring. When I first heard these words, the jury was still out on which path my own life would take. I had learned the ropes of ministry under a handful of seasoned and godly mentors, had held several pastorates in New England and Texas, and had begun to acclimate to the challenging world of Southern California. I was still searching for the particular direction I should take in my own ministry. Honestly, I had no idea *what* God would ultimately do with me. I didn't know exactly *where* He would lead me. But with Schaeffer's words, I was reminded of *how* my ministry should be done—and how it should *not* be done. He wrote, "We must not do the Lord's work in the flesh. We must do the Lord's work in the Lord's way."[2]

Looking back on my early years in the pastorate, it wasn't always easy to distinguish "in the flesh" operation from "by the Spirit" ministry. Youthful confidence, relevant methods, and energetic idealism often led to an "I got this" attitude. But over the years, with a few failures behind me and some real-life experience under my belt, the contrast between serving the Lord in the flesh and serving Him by the power of the Spirit grew increasingly clearer.

Each person has a unique combination of talents, personality, abilities, strengths, resources, and opportunities—believers and unbelievers alike. When we rely on those attributes apart from the power of Christ, we're operating in the energy of our flesh. If you limit your involvement only to familiar activities, or if you never feel stretched beyond your abilities, or if the realms of ministry happen to overlap entirely with your comfort zone, or if you rely on tried-and-true methods and surefire gimmicks to accomplish the tasks before you—*chances are you're operating in the flesh.*

I know I've done that. I'm sure you have too.

When I've relied on the flesh, I've always regretted it later. I've lived long enough to learn the value of doing the Lord's work in the power of Christ. After all, Jesus said, "Apart from me you can do nothing" (John 15:5). Though I've always believed those words, I understand them now better than ever. Without being plugged in to Him as the source of our spiritual power, we'll produce nothing worthwhile, nothing worthy of eternal reward, nothing that will have true, lasting impact. Only the fruit borne by the power of the Spirit in the name of Christ will be deemed authentic.

To do the Lord's work in the Lord's way means we conduct our lives as Christ conducted His. We think as Christ thought. We handle ourselves as Christ handled Himself. We treat people with whom and to whom we minister as Christ did.

All that said, the key characteristic of Spirit-empowered, Christlike ministry?

Humility.

And the key to humility?

Adversity.

You just can't have one without the other.

THE HUMILITY OF CHRIST

When I observe the person and work of Jesus Christ throughout the Gospels, one significant characteristic stands at the center of all the others—humility.

In all my studies I've found only one place where Jesus Christ describes his own inner character or core disposition: "I am humble and gentle at heart" (Matthew 11:29).

Humble. Gentle. Those two words sum up both the Man and His mission. Both are servant terms. To be gentle means to have strength under control. To be humble means to have a lowly disposition—putting others above yourself to serve them in love. That fits Jesus' mission perfectly: "The Son of Man came not to be served but to serve others and to give his life as a ransom for many" (Mark 10:45).

Now recall that God wants all of us to "become like his Son" (Romans 8:29)—to be conformed to His image. In everything we think, say, and do. In our relationships, actions, attitudes, and ministry. God wants us to reflect the qualities Jesus exemplified.

In true humility, the Son came from the very presence of the Father, from the glorious throne of the Godhead, where He had an eternal place as the second person of the triune God. In complete and unconditional humility, He stepped from that heavenly realm of glory into this earthly realm of sin and death. In humility, He took on full humanity, becoming human without losing one particle of divinity. In humility, He suffered and died to save us.

Listen to the words of Paul in what many believe was an early hymn about Christ:

> Though he was God,
>> he did not think of equality with God
>> as something to cling to.
> Instead, he gave up his divine privileges;
>> he took the humble position of a slave
>> and was born as a human being.
> When he appeared in human form,
>> he humbled himself in obedience to God
>> and died a criminal's death on a cross.

PHILIPPIANS 2:6-8

Sit back and think about that! The eternal Son of God didn't clutch His heavenly position and divine prerogatives with self-centered entitlement. Instead, His other-focused love motivated Him to let go of His rightful place, empty Himself of His exalted status, humble Himself as a servant to others, and ultimately endure the most humiliating form of torture and death.

Yet as we rightly ponder the profundity of this theologically rich passage, we shouldn't lose sight of Paul's purpose in reminding his readers of Christ's humility, as stated in the verses right before this portion. Pay attention. In fact, read the following words out loud—slowly. They're the key to doing the Lord's work in the Lord's way:

Don't be selfish; don't try to impress others. Be humble, thinking of others as better than yourselves. Don't look out only for your own interests, but take an interest in others, too.

You must have the same attitude that Christ Jesus had.

PHILIPPIANS 2:3-5

There it is. We're called to think, to be, and to do as Jesus thought, was, and did. When we do the Lord's work in the Lord's way, those are the characteristics of our ministry.

At this point, you may be thinking, "Well, Chuck, that's great advice—for you. But I'm not in the ministry. I don't get paid to do the Lord's work. I get paid to do my work, or my company's work."

Not so fast.

If you know Christ as your Savior and Lord, *you're called to ministry.* You may not be a paid pastor, evangelist, counselor, or missionary, but you're involved in doing the Lord's work. And not just when you're volunteering for a church ministry or charity. In fact, Paul tells believers to serve their earthly masters as they would serve Christ: "Work with enthusiasm, as though you were working for the Lord rather than for people" (Ephesians 6:7).

Regardless of your career, calling, or profession, as a believer you should be marked by gentle humility. You won't be going out of your way to impress others. You won't be constantly seeking your own interests. You don't manipulate people to get your own way. You think about their interests, put them first, seek ways to approach them with a lowly, servant-hearted demeanor. Because all Christians are God's servants in *everything* we do, we are to carry out His work in His way. And, again, what is "His way"?

Christlike humility and gentleness.

SERVING OTHERS WITH HUMILITY

The theme of humility runs through Paul's writings like a golden thread. Just as it was central to Christ's identity and mission, it should be central to our own lives and ministries. Another passage—this time in Paul's letter to the Romans—underscores this principle.

We often think of the book of Romans as a great doctrinal treatise in which Paul probes the depths of the gospel of salvation by grace alone through faith alone in Christ alone. It certainly is that! But when you get to chapter 12, it takes a deliberate turn to the immensely practical. It's as if all the powerful theology of chapters 1 to 11 is fashioned into an arrow and aimed directly at our sinful hearts.

I want Paul's words to minister directly to you, so, again, read these out loud. Take your time. Don't rush through them. Imagine Paul wrote these thoughts to you personally.

Don't think you are better than you really are. Be honest in your evaluation of yourselves, measuring yourselves by the faith God has given us. Just as our bodies have many parts and each part has a special function, so it is with Christ's body. We are many parts of one body, and we all belong to each other. . . .

Don't just pretend to love others. Really love them. Hate what is wrong. Hold tightly to what is good. Love each other with genuine affection, and take delight in honoring each other. . . . When God's people are in need, be ready to help them. Always be eager to practice hospitality.

Bless those who persecute you. Don't curse them; pray that God will bless them. Be happy with those who are happy, and weep with those who weep. Live in harmony with each other. Don't be too proud to enjoy the company of ordinary people. And don't think you know it all!

ROMANS 12:3-5, 9-10, 13-16

Now read those words again, this time at an even slower pace.

When our lives are marked by humility, the attitudes and actions described by Paul will be evident to all. In contrast, the ways of the flesh have nothing in common with these traits. When we operate in the flesh, we tend to look for ways we're superior to others. We exaggerate our own abilities. We flaunt our accomplishments. We tend to be task oriented rather than people centered. We say we love others, but our actions—or *lack* of action—betray us.

In the flesh, we dishonor people, belittle their contributions, manipulate them, dismiss them, and shove them aside when they are no longer useful to us. We boast about our positions and flaunt our titles. We overlook people's needs, keep to ourselves, and refuse to extend a helping hand.

If we're controlled by the flesh, we find ways to exact revenge against those who oppose us, become envious of another's success, and dish out a heap of "I told you so" when others fail. We hang with the powerful, the popular, and the pretty, avoiding people who can't help us get ahead. And we love to parade our knowledge and point out others' ignorance.

None of those qualities reflect the character of Christ. When we imitate Christ in life and ministry, we do it with genuine humility. Few things are worse than phony humility. It reeks of hypocrisy. When humility is real, it disarms people, especially because in a world driven by carnality, very few people expect it.

Consider this: if the God of the universe could step down into our world and exhibit true humility, gentleness, and a servant's mission, why would *we* be off the hook? If anyone had any basis to strut His stuff, it was Jesus. Remember, "The Son of Man came not to be served but to serve others and to give his life as a ransom for many" (Matthew 20:28).

A PICTURE OF LOWLINESS

The somber scene is no doubt familiar to you: the Last Supper.

In keeping with the law and according to centuries of Hebrew tradition, Jesus and the Twelve gather for the Passover meal. It will be their last together. The climax of His earthly mission approaches. As Jesus partakes of the sacrificial lamb, breaks bread, and shares the fruit of the vine with His closest friends, the religious elites in Jerusalem secretly scheme with each other about how to put Him to death. Jesus knows His arrest, trial, torture, and execution are drawing near.

What do you do when you know your time has come? What do you say? With what do you punctuate your life's message?

In John's account of that evening, he spotlights an event the other three Gospel writers leave out of their accounts. While Matthew, Mark, and Luke relay the establishment of the Lord's Supper with the bread and wine as signs of Jesus' broken body and shed blood, John complements their account with an additional scenario. A scenario, I'm sure, that made an impression on John that lasted for decades.

John unpacks the scene with some important reminders about Jesus Himself: "Jesus knew that his hour had come to leave this world and return to his Father. He had loved his disciples during his ministry on earth, and now he loved them to the very end" (John 13:1). What Jesus is about to do during that Passover gathering will be a sure sign of His love for His disciples—the same kind of love we're to show for one another. There was no condition to His love, no limit. He loved each of them to the uttermost. Deeply. Consistently. Sacrificially.

To picture the scene, we need to understand a little background about meals in first-century Judea. Tabletops in those days stood close to the floor, more like a low coffee table than a stately dining room table. People reclined on their sides around the table. They usually had pillows to support them, but they rested on their elbows and ate with their hands. No chairs. No knives and forks. The scene would have been very close and intimate.

Unknown to the other disciples, Judas Iscariot has already made up his mind to betray Jesus (13:2), but they are all still reclining at the table, passing food, chatting, and, as we'll see, even wrangling with each other and ruffling feathers.

What John writes next is vital to understanding the profoundness of what Jesus is about to do: "Jesus knew that the Father had given him authority over everything and that he had come from God and would return to God" (13:3). Think about that. Jesus knew who He was. He was fully aware of His divine nature, His heavenly origin, and His glorious destiny. Imagine what such knowledge would do to somebody operating in the flesh! The flesh would demand total allegiance and obedience. It would require the disciples to wait on Him hand and foot.

Yet Jesus takes the exact opposite route. Knowing full well His rightful position of absolute sovereignty, Jesus "got up from the table, took off his robe, wrapped a towel around his waist, and poured water into a basin. Then he began to wash the disciples' feet, drying them with the towel he had around him" (13:4-5).

From our western, twenty-first-century perspective, it's difficult to imagine the awkwardness of that moment. The fact that their master and teacher stands up from the table likely catches the disciples off guard. *Where's He going? What's He doing?*

When He grabs the implements for washing feet, the strange situation takes a turn toward the bizarre—even the unseemly. In that culture, some might even have called it offensive. If the Queen of

England were to stand up from a state dinner at Buckingham Palace and start clearing dishes, it wouldn't be as shocking as Jesus washing His disciples' feet would have been in His day.

I like to imagine gasps and murmurs among those reclining disciples. Wide eyes all around. Dropped jaws. Maybe a few shaking heads.

Here's one more observation to help us understand the broader context of Jesus' action. The fact that the disciples' feet are still dirty and need washing should strike us as strange. Why? Because in the ancient Near East, guests would usually have removed their sandals at the door, where a servant of the lowest rank would be kneeling to cleanse their feet with a basin of water and a towel. Because the disciples are observing the Passover in a borrowed room, there is apparently no servant on duty that night.

In that case, the disciples have two options. First, each one could wash his own feet. After all, the water and towel are at the door. Or, second, one of them could voluntarily take on the role of the servant and bathe the feet of all the others. Not a chance! Not a single one of them feels compelled to humble himself enough to carry out either option. The task of washing feet was below them. They'd rather cozy up to the table with dirty feet than stoop so low as to clean their own or the others' feet.

To make matters worse, Luke tells us that just a few minutes before Jesus donned the towel, the disciples "began to argue among themselves about who would be the greatest among them" (Luke 22:24). So, with that "me-first" attitude still lingering in the room like a thick stench, Jesus puts everybody else first and takes on the role of a household servant.

PRINCIPLES OF CHRISTLIKE HUMILITY

After meditating on this scene for years, I've noticed four principles about humility we need to keep in mind, especially in our culture that is every bit as "me-first" as in the disciples' day.

Humility Is Unannounced

Notice that Jesus doesn't stand up and declare, "Okay, time out! Enough boasting. I'm going to do something that'll cut you down to size! This is going to be such a great act of humility, you'll never forget it. In fact, John, you might want to take some notes on this. It's gonna be BIG!"

No, that would be shameless pride, not humility. That's the kind of trumpeting of good works the Pharisees had developed into a fine art. Jesus isn't into that kind of proud "virtue-signaling," and neither should we be. Truly humble people don't announce or show off their acts of humility. Jesus stands up without a word, prepares Himself for the lowly task, kneels down, and begins washing feet. His actions speak louder than any lengthy lecture He could deliver on the subject.

Humility Is Willing to Receive

Humble people are also willing to receive from others, without embarrassment or resistance. When Jesus makes it around the table to Peter, that rugged fisherman has obviously been rehearsing what he will do in response. Anything to show up his fellow disciples. After all, the argument over who is the greatest is still rattling around in their brains.

So, when Jesus sets the basin down and takes Peter's foot in his hands, Peter objects: "Lord, are you going to wash my feet?" (John 13:6). We should hear a tone of incredulity in those words.

Jesus replies, "You don't understand now what I am doing, but someday you will" (13:7). Note the absolute patience Jesus shows toward His hardheaded disciples.

Peter then doubles down on His resistance to Jesus' act of grace: "No . . . you will never ever wash my feet!" (13:8).

Peter wants his words to come across as humility, but instead they barely mask a deep-seated pride. He fails to admit his physical and spiritual neediness. He resists Christ's act of grace.

Before we slam Peter for his pride, though, we need to remember that we ourselves sometimes have the same response. We make it hard for people who are trying to help us. We resist when people try to give.

I must confess, I often fall into this trap. That's why I try not to shake my finger or cluck my tongue at Peter's obstinacy. To be honest, I often find it difficult to receive from others. My pride bucks against it. I know I'm not alone in this. A lot of people—especially men—are in the same category.

I was reminded of this problem one Christmas several years ago. A man in our church showed up at our home with a Christmas gift for our family. But this gift wasn't something he could set at our doorstep or place under our tree. No, his gift to us was to wash all the windows in our home.

I wasn't there when he arrived. Cynthia and the kids welcomed him in and let him get started. I showed up from the church office while the man was still at work out back by the patio. My initial response was surprise and a touch of embarrassment. I asked him what he was doing.

"Chuck," he said with a smile, "I just wanted to do this as my gift for you and your family. Merry Christmas!"

My surprise turned to deeper embarrassment. "Hey, thanks. How about you just finish up the patio doors? We'll take care of the rest."

"Nope, I'd like to go all the way around."

My embarrassment became resistance. "That's great, man, but I'm sure you've got much more important things to do. You just do the downstairs, and the kids and I will do the upstairs, okay?"

He shook his head. "No, thanks, I want to do them all."

I kept squabbling with him. I just couldn't stand the thought of his doing all that work for us.

Finally, the man paused, looked me in the eye, and said, "Chuck, I want to wash *ALL* the windows, upstairs and downstairs, inside and outside, every one of them. Listen, you're always giving to everybody else. I'd like you to receive for a change."

At that moment, I realized I was like Peter refusing to let Jesus wash his feet. I understood him. Servanthood was hard for Peter, especially when it called for receiving from someone else. Maybe you have been in the same position—not too humble to give but far too proud to graciously receive.

Needless to say, the man washed all our windows. What a gift!

Humility Is Not a Sign of Weakness

Jesus' response to Peter's resistance is not one of weakness. It sets Peter straight. He doesn't back off. He doesn't capitulate to Peter's self-involved reluctance. When Peter insists that Jesus will never wash his feet, the Lord replies without flinching: "Unless I wash you, you won't belong to me" (John 13:8). Now, we know Jesus is making a deeper theological point. Peter's stubborn pride is a sign of spiritual self-reliance; Jesus offers unconditional mercy and grace. Until dirty sinners allow the holy Son of God to wash them clean, they have no fellowship with Him.

Jesus' reply to Peter reminds us of an important principle. Doing the Lord's work with deep humility doesn't turn you into a spineless wimp. It's not an invitation for people to walk all over you. In fact, true humility makes you a spiritual heavyweight. From His place of utter humility, Jesus stands up to Peter. He calls him out on his nonsense. And look at verse 12: He washes all the disciples' feet.

Even Judas's.

Humility Doesn't Play Favorites

As we read the rest of this chapter, we realize Jesus knows Judas will betray Him. Even in His tug of war with Peter over washing his feet, Jesus hints at this reality: "A person who has bathed all over does not need to wash, except for the feet, to be entirely clean. And you disciples are clean, but not all of you" (John 13:10). John explains what Jesus means by that last line: "For Jesus knew who would betray him. That is what he meant when he said, 'Not all of you are clean'" (verse 11). Isn't that interesting? Even knowing that Judas's heart is still stained with sin and needs the supernatural cleansing of forgiveness, Jesus washes his feet in deep humility.

How easy it is to have favorites in ministry. Believe me, some people are easy to love and to serve. Yes, there's such a thing as a "preacher's pet." They're on the edge of their seat during the sermon. They're the first ones to leap forward when the church asks for help. They're thoughtful, respectful, responsive, caring, and available.

Then there are the Judases. Thankfully, I haven't met as many of them. But I've run across enough. They're shifty eyed. Always seem to be plotting something. Mumbling and grumbling. They cross their arms and lift their noses at the sermon. They don't sing the hymns. They come in late and leave early. They don't get involved, personally, in any ministry, and they complain when they aren't noticed and served.

But true humility serves them all: the intrepid Peters, the tenderhearted Johns, the doubting Thomases, and, yes, even the treacherous Judases. Just as tenderly as Jesus uses the towel to dry Andrew's and Matthew's feet, He dries Judas's feet. Because humility doesn't overlook the unlovely, it doesn't play favorites.

MINISTERING TO OTHERS IN HUMILITY

After washing the disciples' feet, Jesus takes His place again at the table, and like any great teacher, He makes sure they comprehend what He has just done (John 13:12). Even though He is rightfully their great Teacher and sovereign Lord (13:13), He surrenders the prerogatives of those positions and literally takes the role of a servant. It is a perfect picture of the humility of the incarnation described in Philippians 2:7. Remember? "He gave up his divine privileges; he took the humble position of a slave."

After watching Him return to His seat, I'm sure the disciples expect Jesus to request that they wash His feet in return. But He doesn't. Instead of insisting that they pay Him back, He urges them to pay it forward: "Since I, your Lord and Teacher, have washed your feet, you ought to wash each other's feet. I have given you an example to follow. Do as I have done to you" (John 13:14-15).

Most people—even those unfamiliar with the Bible—have heard of the Golden Rule. It comes from Matthew 7:12—"Do to others whatever you would like them to do to you." Jesus' words to His disciples take this principle and center it squarely on His person and work: "Do as I have done to you." Jesus is the Golden Rule incarnate.

In light of Christ's example of humility and His charge to the disciples, I see two important lessons for us.

Ministering in Humility Means Serving One Another

Jesus leaves no room in His example and instruction for loving and serving the Lord without loving and serving others.

Let me state that more directly: Jesus tells us that we love and serve Him *by loving and serving others*. That's the genius of washing one another's feet. Jesus puts it clearly: "Just as I have loved you, you should love each other" (John 13:34). We forgive others because Christ forgave us. We extend grace toward others because Christ showered us with grace. None of us is greater than our Master. If He humbled Himself to serve others, you and I must do likewise.

God Blesses Those Who Demonstrate Humility

God blesses us for actually showing humility, not just for knowing about it. According to Scripture, God has chosen to bless us through specific actions. For example, those who fear the Lord will be blessed (see Psalm 115:13). Those who help the poor will receive blessing (see Proverbs 14:21; 22:9). We receive spiritual blessing when we reflect on the death and resurrection of Jesus through the Lord's Supper (see 1 Corinthians 10:16). We're blessed when we endure testing and temptations (see James 1:12). We're even blessed for reading the words of the book of Revelation (see Revelation 1:3). And the Beatitudes of Jesus' Sermon on the Mount describe specific blessings to the poor and needy, those who mourn, the humble, those who hunger for justice, the merciful, the pure of heart, the peacemakers, and the persecuted (see Matthew 5:3-10).

The fact is, God has attached blessing to certain actions done in sincerity. So, too, in John 13:17, Jesus informs the disciples, "Now that you know these things, God will bless you for doing them." Which things? His example of setting aside our own privileges and prerogatives and clothing ourselves with humility to serve one another—stooping even as low as the least servant tasked with washing dirty feet!

Jesus is saying that knowing His teachings on humility isn't enough. He's looking for action from us, not theory. He doesn't want you to study about humility, to form discussion groups, to meditate on it, or merely to memorize verses about it. He wants you to imitate His selfless, other-centered actions with authentic humility that has nothing to do with personal gain. With those actions comes spiritual blessing.

Are you ready and willing to rest in the omnicapable hands of your loving, sovereign Lord, who wants to lead you into Christlike humility? Then brace yourself for a wild ride of adversity, calamities, trials, and tragedies. But also rest in the blessed knowledge that when you do the Lord's work in the Lord's way—with Christlike humility—your rewards will be many, in this life and in the life to come.

Concluding Thoughts

You may be too young to know the feeling of your wrists resting on the sides of a pinball machine as your fingers work frantically, clacking the flippers and smacking that little silver ball around the playfield.

Or maybe you know exactly what that's like.

Those classic arcade games—with their flashing lights, ringing bells, and thumping bumpers—kept kids (and adults) entertained for decades until they were all but replaced by video consoles and handheld devices. If you've never experienced the classic pinball machine, you need to. At least once.

Even if you've lived fewer years on this blue-and-green orb than I have, I'm sure you can relate to that little silver pinball—suddenly plunged into a rough-and-tumble world, bounced through a labyrinth of challenges, bruised by hardships, tossed around by a cacophony of upheavals, pummeled by tragedies. Without some perspective, we could easily begin to feel like helpless objects stuck in a convoluted maze, trusting that Somebody up there knows what He's doing, hoping all this seemingly hapless commotion is more than just a cosmic game.

Now pause for a moment and recall the litany of life's twists and turns we've covered in the chapters of this book:

- lingering troubles
- unrelieved suffering
- unconfessed sin
- shocking tests
- sudden calamities
- emotional trauma
- intimidating giants
- slashing thorns
- painful discipline
- slammed doors
- unexpected solitude
- pride-crushing adversity

What a list! The longer we live, the more of these we transfer from the category of "I hope that never happens to me" to the category of "been there, done that."

Yet there's no need for us to picture these hardships as bumpers, spinners, flippers, or traps designed to set us off through a dizzying series of random mishaps at the left and right hands of misfortune and chance. Rather, in the hands of an all-powerful, all-knowing, all-loving God, these obstacles of adversity lead the way to Christlikeness. Yes, they have a way of cutting us down to size and bringing us to our knees. But they cultivate true humility in place of arrogance, trust in God rather than independence, and walking in the Spirit instead of self-reliance. By embracing difficulties, we acquire the kind of attitudes that Christ modeled so beautifully.

My fervent prayer is that you *lift your eyes* from that list of trials and troubles. Lift them high.

Not to fallen, frail men and women dealing with their own lists. Higher than that.

Not to some self-help philosophy that lifts you from the ground just long enough for you to plummet back into disappointment.

Lift your eyes much, much higher.

Lift your eyes to the Lord, enthroned in heaven (see Psalm 123:1). Lift them to the One who made heaven and earth (see Psalm 121:2). Fix your eyes on the one who orders chaos, fills emptiness, and lights up the darkness.

When you do, you'll see clearly that there's a purpose at the end of life's journey of adversity.

In fact, *more* than a purpose—there's a *Person*. Trust Him, and He will see you through.

Questions for Reflection and Discussion

CHAPTER 1: WHEN TROUBLES COME AND STAY

1. Think about the biggest trouble in your life that has "come and stayed" in the last year or so. How are you handling that? In light of the principles presented in this chapter, what are you doing right? What could you be doing better?

2. What lesson(s) might God be teaching you through this trouble about Himself? About you? About someone or something else?

3. Read through James 1:2-12 again. Which principles and promises about troubles do you find most encouraging in your present trial? Why do these mean so much to you?

4. If somebody were to ask you what specific blessings of God you are experiencing *now*—in the midst of your troubles—how would you answer?

5. In prayer, ask God for wisdom and endurance through your present struggles and through whatever may come your way. Be specific. If you're working through these questions with someone else, spend time praying for each other's burdens. End with thanksgiving for the promise and provision God gives in the midst of your troubles.

CHAPTER 2: WHEN SUFFERING LEAVES ITS MARK

1. What has been your experience with people claiming to be faith healers or people who believe in the kind of faith healing illustrated at the beginning of this chapter?

2. Review the five foundational facts until you can state them in your own words from memory:

   - There are two categories of sin: original and personal.
   - Original sin introduced sickness and death to humanity.
   - Sometimes there is a direct relationship between personal sins and sickness.
   - Sometimes there is no relationship between the two.
   - It is not God's will that everyone should be healed.

3. Now review the three God-designed purposes for suffering drawn from 2 Corinthians 1:4-11 until you can state them in your own words from memory:

- Suffering gives us opportunity to comfort others.
- Suffering keeps us from trusting in ourselves.
- Suffering teaches us to give thanks in everything.

4. Imagine someone who is suffering with a chronic illness tells you, "I've prayed and prayed for God to take this from me, but it just seems to get worse and worse." Then they ask you the following questions. Based on the principles in this chapter, how would you answer?

- What did I do to deserve this?
- Why won't God heal me? Didn't He promise to heal us if we have enough faith?
- Why is God letting this happen to me?

CHAPTER 3: WHEN GOD HEALS BODY AND SOUL

1. Explain, in your own words, the difference between "common grace" and "special grace" as these two categories relate to God's chosen methods of healing.

2. Review the erroneous beliefs about healing. Which of these have you been taught or believed in the past? How would you respond to those misconceptions today?

3. Share a personal experience in which you endured long-term suffering or sickness from which God later delivered you. What did you learn about God and yourself through the suffering? What did you learn through the recovery?

4. After Job lost everything he owned and virtually everyone he loved in a series of unprecedented tragedies, he declared, "But he knows where I am going. And when he tests me, I will come out as pure as gold. . . . He will do to me whatever he has planned" (Job 23:10, 14). How does Job's perspective expressed in these words compare to the way you tend to respond to the trials and tragedies God allows in your life?

5. Of the four practical principles for reframing our perspective on sickness and healing—confess, pray, seek, and thank—which do you most urgently need to apply in your current circumstances?

CHAPTER 4: WHEN UNEXPECTED TESTS RATTLE OUR WORLD

1. What was the most recent or memorable time of trial and testing you've been through in your life? Was it more of a "sudden burst" or a "slow burn"?

2. Evaluate and explain your response to this test on a grading scale from A to F. In your response to the trial, what did you "get right"? What did you "get wrong"?

3. God doesn't always reveal the specific purpose of the times of testing He allows into your life, but sometimes He does. Looking back again at the trial you endured, did God somehow reveal the purpose behind it? If God was urging you to release an item or person you were clutching too tightly, what or who was it?

4. In your own words, how was Abraham able to obey God's seemingly absurd command to offer Isaac as a sacrifice? What foundational elements of his theology (beliefs about God) contributed to his response?

5. Thinking about your answers to the previous question, how do those beliefs about God apply to your own time of testing? How might they allow you to look at that trial in a different light?

6. Finally, is there anything you are clinging to right now—people, plans, possessions, or positions—that God might want you to loosen your grip on and hold with open hands? Spend some time in prayer working through that possibility with God. This exercise can be challenging and emotional, and it can take weeks or years, instead of a few minutes. So don't rush through it. Take your time.

CHAPTER 5: WHEN CALAMITY CRASHES IN

1. When you close your eyes and picture Job, what do you see? A man marred by crisis and calamity or a man marked by integrity and prosperity? If somebody were to picture you, how might they imagine your portrait—frowning and fretting in worry and complaint or standing strong in the midst of life's inevitable hardships?

2. Think about a time when sudden, shocking calamity came crashing into your life. Do you feel you were prepared or unprepared for it? Evaluate your words, attitudes, and actions throughout that calamity.

3. Put yourself in the place of Job. Based on the experience you considered in the last question, how do you think you would have responded to the extreme catastrophes he endured? Jot down some words that might describe your response or even some phrases you might utter. Be painfully honest.

4. Now put yourself in the place of a close friend of somebody going through the kind of tragic loss Job suffered. What is your tendency in such situations? To stay away? To remain silent? To sermonize? To cast blame? Try to recall a recent response to such a situation.

5. Now consider the practical applications for surviving when calamity crashes in. Which of these truths are most firmly fixed in your mind? Which might need some foundation work? How might you have fared differently in your own time of calamity if these truths had all been in place?

   - Our trials are inevitable; don't be surprised.
   - Our friends are fallible; don't be fooled.
   - Our God is sovereign; don't be disillusioned.

CHAPTER 6: WHEN GOD GIVES GRACE TO ENDURE

1. Many people bear the permanent scars of abuse, trauma, and catastrophe. These things affect some of us on a daily basis. They can be difficult even to think about, much less to discuss with others. Even being prompted to probe those past pains can feel like a punch in the gut when we're on the long journey of recovery. In light of this reality, what are

your initial reactions to the doctrine of God's sovereignty and abiding presence even through those times of acute pain? Why might it be difficult to accept that He is present even in those calamities? How may this doctrine be comforting to you?

2. Consider a circumstance in which it seemed clear that God had positioned you in the right place at the right time, when everything seemed to click, and you realized He had brought you to that moment for a purpose. Now think back to the string of events that brought you to that point—difficult decisions, painful experiences, hardships, victories, defeats. What does this reveal about how God works things out in our lives according to His plan? How should this affect the way we think about our current and future trials?

3. Because of Joseph's theology of God's sovereignty, he was able not only to endure trauma but to forgive the wickedness of his brothers. Read Genesis 50:14-21. Put yourself in the place of Joseph's brothers. In what ways do you find their fears understandable? Then put yourself in the place of Joseph. In your own words, how would you defend his attitude of forgiveness and kindness?

4. What strained relationships in your own life come closest to that of Joseph and his brothers? In light of God's providential grace, what practical changes might you need to make in your attitudes, words, and actions?

5. The three pillars of Joseph's theology enabled him to endure abuse and trauma. Strengthen these pillars in your own life by

meditating on the following passages of Scripture. Describe how they apply to the kinds of situations and strained relationships you've considered in the preceding questions.

- See God's perfect plan in every location. (Study Psalm 139:5, 7-10.)
- Sense God's gracious hand in every position. (Study 1 Samuel 2:6-8; 1 Peter 5:6.)
- Submit to God's sovereign will in every situation. (Study Romans 8:28.)

CHAPTER 7: WHEN THE GIANTS OF LIFE ATTACK

1. Name your giant. What challenge are you facing today that seems too overwhelming to handle?

2. Spend a few minutes thinking about how you've been trying to face this giant. What strategies have you employed, and what steps have you taken so far with this challenge? How have those worked?

3. What voices are you listening to about this giant? These voices may be your own thoughts on the matter—or well-meaning naysayers telling you what can't be done. Weigh those thoughts and opinions carefully. What weaknesses of your giant might you have overlooked? What strengths might you have exaggerated?

4. Relay a "lion and bear" story or two of how God has delivered you from past giants. How did He do it? What was your role in

that deliverance? What does this teach you about how God can and does act on your behalf?

5. Through our faith in Christ, God has equipped us with His Spirit. Meditate on the following passages of Scripture and consider how each can give you the faith, confidence, and strength you need to go toe-to-toe with your own giant.

- Galatians 5:22-23
- Ephesians 6:10-17
- 2 Timothy 1:7
- 1 John 4:4

CHAPTER 8: WHEN THORNS RIP OUR PRIDE

When thorns rip at our pride, it's normal to recoil, like pulling our hand away from an open flame or swatting away a biting fly. Instead, let's take some time to focus our attention on the perennial problem of pride and the principles of purifying pain. To do this, I want you to think through ten self-diagnostic questions in response to the lessons of 2 Corinthians 12. Don't rush through them. Ponder them. Turn them over in your mind. Discuss them with people close to you. Then take the appropriate action before God and others.

1. Is your self-image too important to you?

2. Do you spend too much time and energy trying to impress those around you?

3. Does someone else's opinion of you mean too much? Whose? Why?

4. Are you easily offended by someone's negative comments about you or to you?

5. How well do you model in your own life what you expect in another's life?

6. Do you give other people the credit they deserve, or do you tend to take credit for things others do for you?

7. Are you vulnerable to others, quick to acknowledge your weaknesses and mistakes instead of being defensive or secretive?

8. When you know you don't know, do you say you don't know, or do you pretend you do?

9. Do you secretly keep score regarding your achievements, especially comparing them to others' wins?

10. When you suffer, do you focus on the pain it brings or the lessons it teaches?

I'm assuming you know how each of those questions *should* be answered. Chances are, pride plagues you like it does most people. What "thorns in the flesh" do you feel the Lord has brought into your life to treat this universal and ongoing condition? Acknowledge this to God, and ask Him for His sufficient grace to give you strength to endure.

CHAPTER 9: WHEN GOD'S DISCIPLINE STRIKES

1. When you hear the word *discipline*, what kinds of positive and negative thoughts come to mind? What has been your personal

experience of discipline as a child growing up or perhaps as a parent with your own children? How might your experiences of discipline affect your attitude toward God's discipline of His children?

2. How would you describe the similarities and differences between your experiences of parental discipline and God's discipline in our lives?

3. In your own words, describe why God's discipline in our lives—though painful—is beneficial for us.

4. Of the following attitudes and actions against which Paul explicitly warns his readers in 1 Corinthians 10, which one or two are most relevant for you?

- Craving evil things (covetousness, envy)
- Putting other things before God (idolatry, materialism)
- Sexual impurity (lust, fornication, adultery, pornography)
- Putting God to the test (ingratitude, presuming on God's grace)
- Grumbling against authority (complaining, rebelling, criticizing)

5. Take time to confess the attitudes and actions you identified. Be specific. Bring them to the Lord and claim His forgiving grace and ongoing mercy. But don't stop there. Thank the Lord for His faithful warnings as well as His hand of constructive and corrective discipline that help to conform us to the image of His Son.

CHAPTER 10: WHEN DOORS SLAM SHUT

1. Describe a time when you made big plans to head in a certain direction in life or ministry, but the Lord slammed the door closed on that pursuit. How did that feel? How did you respond?

2. Looking back, what other door of opportunity did the Lord open instead?

3. Consider your current "limitations." What doors seem to be closed to you right now?

4. Answer the question, "Given my current circumstances, what could I have done for Christ *last* year?" Come up with at least three answers. Then answer this question: "Given my current circumstances, what can I do for Christ *this* year?" Come up with at least three answers. Maybe you've been asked to do something in church or in another ministry, but you've said no. Could this be an invitation to step through an open door?

5. Commit to following through on at least one of your answers in the previous question.

CHAPTER 11: WHEN SOLITUDE DRIVES US DEEPER

1. Do you like being alone? If so, what three aspects do you like about it? If not, what three aspects do you dislike?

2. Would you consider yourself more of a people person or a task-oriented person? How does this orientation help or hinder your need for silence and solitude?

3. If somebody were to ask you why solitude is important for our spiritual health, what would you tell them based on this chapter? To what biblical examples or principles could you point?

4. In the past few months, has the Lord "forced" you into unexpected aloneness—or at least a slower pace? What did He teach you through this season of solitude? What, if anything, did you discover about yourself, about others, or about God?

5. What's keeping you from setting aside frequent times of silence and solitude? Plan on taking time at least once a week for this important discipline, and consider when and where it will take place.

CHAPTER 12: WHEN ADVERSITY LEADS TO HUMILITY

1. Who is the humblest person you've ever known? What specific words, attitudes, or actions does that person exhibit that mark him or her as humble?

2. Study the following passages, then describe some benefits of humility: Proverbs 11:2; 15:33; 22:4; James 3:13; 1 Peter 5:5.

3. What kinds of actions would demonstrate the opposite of humility? Describe at least five. Which of these do you tend to exhibit the most in your interactions with others?

4. Do you find it more difficult to give to others or to receive from others? How do each of these stem from a lack of humility?

5. In most cultures in the modern world, washing a guest's feet isn't routinely practiced. However, other "lowly" acts toward family members, friends, or even strangers would be cultural equivalents in our own day. Discuss some menial tasks you can do for others as acts of humility that you might be tempted to think are "below you." Make a plan to follow Jesus' example and do as He has done for you.

Acknowledgments

I'M INDEBTED TO SEVERAL IMPORTANT people in my life who assisted me in getting this book into your hands.

First, I'm grateful for my friend and outstanding editor, Dr. Michael Svigel. Mike is not only a clear-thinking theologian and much-respected professor of theology at Dallas Seminary, he's a superb writer with a keen eye and an understanding heart. It has been a pleasure to work with him during these many months, which have included the ongoing COVID-19 pandemic and all sorts of trials and challenges. But he diligently endured!

Second, I want to express my thanks to Jon Farrar and Stephanie Rische, along with several of their colleagues at Tyndale House Publishers, as they have worked together to get this book into print.

Third, once again, I thank my long-time friends Sealy and

Matt Yates for their personal affirmation, wise advice, and professional assistance as my literary agents. Our relationship continues to be edifying and gratifying.

Finally, I must include my wife, Cynthia, who has been in my life throughout our sixty-six years of marriage, as we have endured countless times of testing and, far more often, days of harmony and great delight. As I wrote this book, I underwent a surgical procedure called a partial cornea implant, which required my writing many of these pages using only one eye, a very bright lamp, and a thick magnifying glass. That was a first for me as an author! I'm sure I would not have made it to the end had it not been for the faithful, loving presence and encouragement of "Nurse Cynthia."

Chuck Swindoll
Frisco, Texas

Notes

CHAPTER 1: WHEN TROUBLES COME AND STAY

1. William Shakespeare, *The Comedy of Errors*, Act 2, Scene 1.
2. Malcolm Muggeridge, *A Twentieth Century Testimony* (Nashville: Thomas Nelson, 1978), 18.
3. Daniel Krauthammer, "Eulogy for Charles Krauthammer," in Charles Krauthammer, *The Point of It All: A Lifetime of Great Loves and Endeavors,* updated ed. (New York: Crown Forum, 2019), 330.

CHAPTER 2: WHEN SUFFERING LEAVES ITS MARK

1. See R. Kent Hughes and Bryan Chapell, *1 & 2 Timothy and Titus: To Guard the Deposit,* Preaching the Word (Wheaton, IL: Crossway, 2000), 134.
2. Philip Yancey, *Where Is God When It Hurts?* (Grand Rapids: Zondervan, 1990), 260–261.

CHAPTER 3: WHEN GOD HEALS BODY AND SOUL

1. Martin Luther, "Whether One May Flee from a Deadly Plague (1527)," in Timothy F. Lull and William R. Russell, eds., *Martin Luther's Basic Theological Writings*, 3rd ed. (Minneapolis: Augsburg Fortress, 2012), 482–483.
2. Luther, 483.
3. Millard J. Erickson, *The Concise Dictionary of Christian Theology,* rev. ed. (Wheaton, IL: Crossway, 2001), 82.

4. Joni Eareckson Tada, *A Place of Healing: Wrestling with the Mysteries of Suffering, Pain, and God's Sovereignty* (Colorado Springs: David C. Cook, 2010), 16.
5. Eareckson Tada, 16–17.
6. Colleen Swindoll Thompson, *Reframing Life: Focusing on God When Life Gets Sideways,* rev. ed. (Frisco, TX: IFL Publishing House, 2018).
7. *Institutes* 2.215, in John Calvin, *Institutes of the Christian Religion,* vol. 1, trans. Henry Beveridge (Edinburgh: The Calvin Translation Society, 1845), 317–318.

CHAPTER 4: WHEN UNEXPECTED TESTS RATTLE OUR WORLD
1. Winston Churchill, "Address to the House of Commons," November 12, 1940, International Churchill Society, https://winstonchurchill.org/resources/speeches /1940-the-finest-hour/neville-chamberlain/.
2. Oswald Chambers, *My Utmost for His Highest: Selections for the Year* (Grand Rapids: Oswald Chambers Publications, 1986), May 8.
3. Chambers, May 30.
4. Don Moen, "Jehovah-Jireh," *Give Thanks (Live),* (Integrity's Hosanna! Music, 1986).

CHAPTER 5: WHEN CALAMITY CRASHES IN
1. See Shawn Ley, "Lyon Township Family Who Lost Home in Plane Crash Receives Overwhelming Support from Community," ClickOnDetroit, January 5, 2021, https://www.clickondetroit.com/news/local/2021/01/06/lyon-township-family-who -lost-home-in-plane-crash-receives-overwhelming-support-from-community/.
2. Rabbi Jesse Paikin, "Toto, I Have a Feeling We're Not in Kansas Anymore" (blog), https://jessepaikin.com/tag/wizard-of-oz/.
3. Warren W. Wiersbe, *The Wiersbe Bible Commentary: Old Testament* (Colorado Springs: David C. Cook, 2007), 826.
4. Robert L. Alden, *Job,* The New American Commentary, vol. 11 (Nashville: Broadman & Holman, 1993), 67.

CHAPTER 6: WHEN GOD GIVES GRACE TO ENDURE
1. Frederick Buechner, "Grace," Quote of the Day, May 7, 2018, https://www.frederick buechner.com/quote-of-the-day/2018/5/7/grace.

CHAPTER 7: WHEN THE GIANTS OF LIFE ATTACK
1. Malcolm Gladwell, *David and Goliath: Underdogs, Misfits, and the Art of Battling Giants* (New York: Little, Brown and Company, 2013), 8. For much of the information in this chapter, I am indebted to Gladwell's insightful and inspiring description of the battle between David and Goliath.
2. William L. Lane, "Arms and Warfare," *Baker Encyclopedia of the Bible,* ed. Walter A. Elwell (Grand Rapids: Baker, 1988), 173. For a similar discussion of ancient warfare, see Gladwell, *David and Goliath,* 9-10.
3. W. Emery Barnes, "Sling," *A Dictionary of the Bible Dealing with Its Language, Literature, and Contents Including the Biblical Theology,* ed. James Hastings et al. (Edinburgh: T. & T. Clark, 1911–1912), 553. Also see Gladwell, *David and Goliath,* 9-10.

4. Robert E. Dohrenwend, "The Sling: Forgotten Firepower of Antiquity," in *Dohrenwend's Masterwork on the Spear, Sling, Sai, and Walking Stick: An Anthology of Articles from the Journal of Asian Martial Arts*, ed. Michael A. DeMarco (Santa Fe, NM: Via Media, 2015), 12.

5. Dohrenwend, 13.

6. Gladwell, *David and Goliath*, 9–10.

7. Gladwell, 11.

8. For a similar discussion of the clues to Goliath's weaknesses, see Gladwell, 13-14.

9. "Acromegaly," Mayo Clinic, https://www.mayoclinic.org/diseases-conditions/acromegaly/symptoms-causes/syc-20351222 (accessed 14 June 2021). See also Gladwell, *David and Goliath*, 14.

10. "Gigantism," UCLA Health, http://pituitary.ucla.edu/resources (accessed 14 June 2021).

11. Gladwell, *David and Goliath*, 14–15.

12. Gladwell, 15.

CHAPTER 8: WHEN THORNS RIP OUR PRIDE

1. C. S. Lewis, *The Problem of Pain* (New York: Macmillan, 1962), 83.

2. See Philip Edgcumbe Hughes, *Paul's Second Epistle to the Corinthians* (Grand Rapids: Eerdmans, 1962), 442–448.

3. Frederick William Danker, ed., *A Greek-English Lexicon of the New Testament and Other Early Christian Literature*, 3rd ed. (Chicago: University of Chicago Press, 2000), 930.

4. Danker, 765.

5. Martin Luther, *Luther's Epistle Sermons: Epiphany, Easter and Pentecost,* vol. 2, trans. John Nicholas Lenker and others, Luther's Complete Works, vol. 8 (Minneapolis: Luther Press, 1909), 117.

CHAPTER 9: WHEN GOD'S DISCIPLINE STRIKES

1. Frédéric Louis Godet, *Commentary on First Corinthians* (1889; reprint, Grand Rapids: Kregel, 1977), 487–488.

CHAPTER 10: WHEN DOORS SLAM SHUT

1. Frederick William Danker, ed., *A Greek-English Lexicon of the New Testament and Other Early Christian Literature*, 3rd ed. (Chicago: University of Chicago Press, 2000), 269.

2. Alan Johnson, "Revelation," in *Hebrews–Revelation*, vol. 12 of The Expositor's Bible Commentary, ed. Frank E. Gaebelein and J. D. Douglas (Grand Rapids: Zondervan, 1981), 452.

3. G. B. Caird, *The Revelation of Saint John*, Black's New Testament Commentary, ed. Henry Chadwick (London: A & C Black, 1966; reprint, Peabody, Mass.: Hendrickson, 1999), 51–53.

CHAPTER 11: WHEN SOLITUDE DRIVES US DEEPER

1. Malcolm Muggeridge, *Christ and the Media* (Vancouver: Regent College Publishing, 1977), 25.

2. R. Kent Hughes, *Disciplines of a Godly Man,* updated ed. (Wheaton, IL: Crossway, 2019), 20.
3. F. B. Meyer, *Paul: A Servant of Jesus Christ* (New York: Revell, 1897), 66.
4. Meyer, 67–68.

CHAPTER 12: WHEN ADVERSITY LEADS TO HUMILITY
1. Francis Schaeffer, *No Little People,* reprint ed. (Downers Grove, IL: InterVarsity, 1974; reprint, Wheaton, IL: Crossway, 2003), 63.
2. Schaeffer, 75.

About the Author

CHARLES R. SWINDOLL is the founder and senior pastor–teacher of Stonebriar Community Church in Frisco, Texas. But Chuck's listening audience extends far beyond a local church body, as *Insight for Living* airs on major Christian radio markets around the world. Chuck's extensive writing ministry has also served the body of Christ worldwide, and his leadership as president and now chancellor emeritus of Dallas Theological Seminary has helped prepare and equip a new generation of men and women for ministry. Chuck and his wife, Cynthia, his partner in life and ministry, have four grown children, ten grandchildren, and seven great-grandchildren.